# WordPerfect® for Windows™ Quick Reference

Margaret D. Hobbie

# Que Quick Reference Series

The *Que Quick Reference Series* is a portable resource of essential microcomputer knowledge. Drawing on the experience of many of Que's best-selling authors, this series helps you easily access important program information. The *Que Quick Reference Series* includes these titles:

*1-2-3 for DOS Release 2.3 Quick Reference*
*1-2-3 for DOS Release 3.1+ Quick Reference*
*1-2-3 for Windows Quick Reference*
*1-2-3 Release 2.2 Quick Reference*
*Allways Quick Reference*
*AutoCAD Quick Reference*, 2nd Edition
*Batch Files and Macros Quick Reference*
*CheckFree Quick Reference*
*CorelDRAW! Quick Reference*
*dBASE IV Quick Reference*
*Excel for Windows Quick Reference*
*Fastback Quick Reference*
*Hard Disk Quick Reference*
*Harvard Graphics 3 Quick Reference*
*LapLink Quick Reference*
*Microsoft Word 5 Quick Reference*
*Microsoft Word Quick Reference*
*Microsoft Works Quick Reference*
*MS-DOS 5 Quick Reference*
*MS-DOS Quick Reference*
*Norton Utilities 6 Quick Reference*
*Paradox 3.5 Quick Reference*
*PC Tools 7 Quick Reference*
*Q&A 4 Quick Reference*
*QuarkXPress 3.1 Quick Reference*
*Quattro Pro Quick Reference*
*Quicken 5 Quick Reference*
*System 7 Quick Reference*
*UNIX Programmer's Quick Reference*
*UNIX Shell Commands Quick Reference*
*Windows 3 Quick Reference*
*WordPerfect 5.1 Quick Reference*
*WordPerfect for Windows Quick Reference*
*WordPerfect Quick Reference*

**Publisher**

Lloyd J. Short

**Production Editor**

Cindy Morrow

**Technical Editor**

Gary Karasik

**Production Team**

Mark Enochs, Brook A. Farling, Sandy Grieshop, Audra Hershman, Betty Kish, Phil Kitchel, Bob LaRoche, John Sleeva, Christine Young

# Table of Contents

# Introduction

*WordPerfect for Windows Quick Reference* is a
collection of the most essential commands and functions
in WordPerfect for Windows, assembled in a quick
reference format. Use it to learn procedures as you learn
the program. Keep it handy to refresh your memory in
procedures that you use infrequently. This book includes
numerous notes, reminders, and cautions to keep you
out of trouble and show you easier ways to accomplish
tasks.

*WordPerfect for Windows Quick Reference* is not
intended to replace comprehensive documentation.
It is more like an unabridged dictionary of common
procedures. For more detailed instruction, see Que's
*Using WordPerfect for Windows* or *WordPerfect for
Windows QuickStart*.

If you are new to the Windows environment, begin by
familiarizing yourself with such features as Link DDE,
Clipboard, dialog boxes, and mouse functions to get
the most out of WordPerfect for Windows. For more
detailed information about Windows 3.0, see Que's
*Using Windows 3,* 2nd Edition.

# Hints For Using This Book

*WordPerfect for Windows Quick Reference* shows you how to perform primary tasks. The Command Reference is the heart of the book. Each command and function is arranged in alphabetical order for easy access. Each topic contains a brief explanation of its purpose, followed by instructions that are broken down by steps. The book is task-oriented, which means that you can look up the task in question rather than having to read through the entire book.

Keep the following conventions in mind when using this book:

- Keys that you press or letters that you type appear in boldface blue type. For example,

  Type **WPWIN** at the prompt.

- On-screen information and messages appear in a special typeface. For example,

  The message `Do you want to save this file?` appears.

- If you see two keys separated by a plus sign, such as

  Press **Shift+F12**

  press and hold the first key, press the second key, and then release both keys.

- If you see two keys separated by a comma, such as

  Press **F12, Enter**

  press and release the first key, and then press and release the second key.

Where applicable, the text points out alternate methods for accomplishing tasks.

# A WORDPERFECT FOR WINDOWS OVERVIEW

WordPerfect for Windows is a powerful word processing program that enables you not only to create documents, but to format, layout, and enhance those documents.

WordPerfect for Windows provides the excellent word processing features that WordPerfect users have enjoyed for years. To these, it adds many new features, some that are made possible by the Windows environment. The following chart provides a brief summary of the new features:

| New Feature | Summary |
| --- | --- |
| Auto Code Placement | If on, automatically places certain codes at the beginning of the page or paragraph. |
| Button Bar | A menu bar of buttons containing commands and macros that offer a fast way to select commands. You can customize the Button Bar for easy access to the commands and macros you use most often. |
| Clipboard | A Windows feature that WordPerfect uses to cut, copy, and paste or append data between applications and documents. |
| FileManager | Takes care of necessary file maintenance, file Quick Lists, changing directories, and so on. |
| Graphics | Now fully mouseable so that you can select, move, or resize graphics by using the mouse. A Viewer enables you to see graphics on disk before you import them. |

| *New Feature* | *Summary* |
|---|---|
| Help | Offers on-line, context-sensitive help for any function. It includes an Index, Glossary, "What Is?" feature, and "How Do I?" feature. |
| Link | A Windows feature that enables you to link a WordPerfect document to another application. Changes that you make in the other application are updated to your WordPerfect document automatically. |
| New Macro Facility | Features a new macro language and a record and play dialog box. |
| Preferences | Enables you to customize WordPerfect with your favorite default settings and preferred working environment. |
| Print Preview | Provides true WYSIWYG (what you see is what you get) if you have added a font package with scaleable fonts. |
| Print Windows Drivers | Enables you to use printer drivers for either Windows or WordPerfect for Windows. You can change the selected drivers in Printer Setup. |
| Ruler | Provides a shortcut for applying formatting options. You can specify whether or not the Ruler appears on-screen. |
| Save As | Saves a file in another format or with a new name. |
| Select | Selects text. You begin by clicking at the beginning of the text that you want to select, holding down the left mouse button, dragging the mouse |

| New Feature | Summary |
|---|---|
| | to highlight the text that you want to include, and then releasing the mouse button. This command is similar to the Block command in WordPerfect 5.1. |
| Windows Interface | Provides fully mouseable menus, dialog boxes, CUA (Common User Access) Keyboard, and the ability to work in up to nine document windows simultaneously. |

# USING A MOUSE

WordPerfect for Windows is fully mouseable. If you do not yet have a mouse, consider investing in one; a mouse can speed up your work significantly. Also, unless you use a mouse, you will miss out on the power of Button Bars, one of the exceptional additions in this newest version of WordPerfect.

The following terms apply to using a mouse in WordPerfect for Windows:

| Term | Definition |
|---|---|
| click | Press and release the left mouse button. |
| double-click | Click twice in rapid succession. |
| triple-click | Click three times in rapid succession. |
| quadruple-click | Click four times in rapid succession. |
| drag | Press and hold down the left mouse button while moving the mouse. |

| Term | Definition |
|------|------------|
| point | Move the mouse until the tip of the insertion point is on an item. |
| insertion point | Mouse pointer that looks like an I-beam; used in text editing. |
| hourglass icon | Mouse pointer that signifies that you should wait for an action. |
| single arrow | Mouse pointer that you use to select menu options. |
| double arrow | Mouse pointer used for moving dialog boxes; appears when you move the insertion point over the title bar of the dialog box. |
| question pointer | Mouse pointer that appears when you press Shift+F1 to get "What Is" Help on any item. |
| hand icon | Mouse pointer that indicates a hand pushing a button. This icon appears on the Button Bar when you add or delete a button. |
| four directional | Mouse pointer that looks like a grappling hook and is used for moving graphics around on the page. |

# SELECTING MENU ITEMS

You can select menu items several ways. The easiest way is to use the mouse. WordPerfect does, however, provide an easy way for you to select items using the keyboard. This keyboard technique is called *Mnemonics*.

# Using the Mouse

The mouse enables you to select menu items easily.
Follow either of these techniques:

- Click on the menu that contains the item that you want to select. Then click the item.

- Move the insertion point to the menu that contains the item you want to select. Press and hold down the mouse button as you drag it to highlight the item that you want. Then release the mouse button.

# Using Mnemonics

Mnemonics are memory aids. In WordPerfect, they help you remember certain keyboard commands. To use Mnemonics to help you access the menus, press Alt to activate the menu bar; then press the underlined letter in the menu name. For example, to pull down the Tools menu, which appears on-screen as

Tools

you would press Alt+T. To select the Speller from the Tools menu, which appears as

Speller

you would then press S. Press Esc to close the menu without making a selection.

# DOCUMENT WINDOWS

With WordPerfect for Windows, you can open up to eight additional document windows, one on top of the other, and switch back and forth between documents.

### *To open a document window*

You can use the following methods for opening a document window:

- Select File, New by clicking with the mouse.
- Press Alt+F, N.
- Press Shift+F4.

### *To use the mouse to switch to another document window*

1. From the menu bar, click Window.
2. Select another document listed in the task list.

### *To use the keyboard to switch to another document window*

1. Press Alt+W to open the Window menu.
2. Press ↓ to highlight the window you want to switch to. You also can press Ctrl+F6 to cycle through the task list.
3. Press Enter to accept your choice. Press Esc to exit the Window menu without making a selection.

# Title and Menu Bars

The title bar at the top of a document window tells you which document you are working on currently. The menu bar, which is located below the title bar, contains pull-down menus for the various commands and functions. Selecting an option that ends with an ellipsis (...) causes a dialog box to appear. Selecting an option that ends with an arrow causes another pull-down menu with additional options to appear.

# Scroll Bars

At the right side of the screen is a scroll bar containing an up arrow, a down arrow, and a scroll button. Use the mouse and the scroll bar to scroll back and forth in your document.

### To display the scroll bar at the bottom of the screen

1. Select File, Preferences, Display. The Display Settings dialog box opens.

2. Select Horizontal Scroll Bar by clicking with the mouse. You also can press Tab until you access the item, and then press the space bar.

3. Select OK to confirm your choice.

### To use the scroll bar

You can use the scroll bar several different ways:

- Click the up or down arrow on the scroll bar to move up and down in the document.

- Position the insertion point on the scroll button while holding down the left mouse button; then move the insertion point up and down in the document.

# Status Bar

At the bottom of the screen is a status bar with changing messages. The message on the right tells you the page number, line number, and insertion point position on the page. The message on the left shows the initial font until you access one of the commands or functions, or change the font. It then displays a new message to explain the option you chose or to list the new font.

# Dialog Boxes

Dialog boxes offer information, messages, options, and warnings, and they enable you to tell the software how to set up certain items. Dialog boxes appear when you select, from a pull-down menu, an item that is followed by an ellipsis (...).

Some dialog boxes, however, appear automatically. If you close a document without first saving it, for example, a dialog box appears to ask whether you want to save the changes to the document. Dialog boxes also often appear when you make a mistake within WordPerfect.

### To use the mouse to navigate through a dialog box

You can use the following mouse techniques within a dialog box:

- Select options by moving the insertion point to the options and clicking the mouse.

- To enter text into text boxes, move the insertion point to the text box, click the mouse, and type the text.

- Click a menu name and hold down the left mouse button. Move the insertion point down the pull-down menu that appears and highlight your choice from the menu; then release the mouse button.

- Move the insertion point to the check box of an option that you want to turn on or off. Click the check box. A check mark in the box indicates that an option is on.

   To turn off a checked item, click the check box again.

- Click OK to save and activate options.

- Click Cancel to close the box without making a selection.

### *To use the keyboard to navigate through a dialog box*

You can use the following keyboard techniques within a dialog box:

- When the dialog box opens, the cursor automatically is positioned on the first item. Press **Tab** to move to the item you want. Press the **space bar** to check or uncheck a check box item or to pop up a "list" menu on dialog box buttons that offer choices. Press **Tab** to move the cursor from option button to option button, and press **Shift+Tab** to move it to the preceding option.

- Press **Tab** to move to a different option.

- Press **Shift+Tab** to move to a previous option.

- Press the **space bar** to select and deselect options in check boxes or to pop up a list on the buttons.

- Use ↓ and ↑ to select items in a list box or to move around a set of options.

- Select commands and menu options by pressing and holding the **Alt** key and pressing the underlined letter of the command or option.

- Press **Enter** to accept your changes and close the dialog box.

### *To move a dialog box with a mouse*

1. Position the mouse pointer over the title bar of the dialog box until the mouse pointer turns into a double arrow.

2. Hold down the left mouse button and drag the dialog box to another part of the screen.

### *To move a dialog box with the keyboard*

1. Press **Alt,**↓ to open the control menu.

2. Press **Enter** to select Move.

3. With the double arrow icon over the title bar, use the arrow keys to move the dialog box. The box moves in the direction of the arrow key that you are pressing.

# Keyboard Techniques

Although using a mouse is often the easiest way to move through WordPerfect, you can navigate through your document using the keyboard. Use the following keys to move around the document:

| Keystroke | Action |
|-----------|--------|
| **Home** | Cursor moves to beginning of line. |
| **End** | Cursor moves to end of line. |
| **Ctrl+Home** | Cursor moves to beginning of document. |
| **Ctrl+End** | Cursor moves to end of document. |
| ↑ | Cursor moves up one line. |
| ↓ | Cursor moves down one line. |
| ← | Cursor moves one character to the left. |
| → | Cursor moves one character to the right. |
| **Ctrl+←** | Cursor moves one word to the left. |
| **Ctrl+→** | Cursor moves one word to the right. |
| **PgUp** | Cursor moves up one page. |
| **PgDn** | Cursor moves down one page. |

# COMMAND REFERENCE

The following section is an alphabetical collection of tasks and procedures in WordPerfect. Step-by-step instructions appear under the appropriate headings.

## Adding Text

### *Purpose*

Enables you to add text to existing text.

## *Insert Mode*

Insert mode inserts new text at the insertion point. Existing text moves forward to make room for new text.

### *To add text in Insert mode*

1. Position the insertion point where you want to add text.

2. Type the new text. Existing text moves to the right.

## *Typeover mode*

Typeover mode replaces existing text with new text that you type. Existing text does not move forward in this mode. If you type **too** when you mean to type **two**, for example, select Typeover mode to replace the first *o* in *two* with a *w*.

### *To type over existing text in Typeover mode*

1. Position the insertion point where you want the new text to begin.

2. Press **Ins** to turn off Insert mode.

3. Type the new text over the old text.

4. Press **Ins** to restore Insert mode.

# Advance

## *Purpose*

Moves text to a different position on the page. You can
advance text up, down, left, or right.

## *To advance text or graphics*

1. Select Layout, Advance.  A dialog box opens.

2. Use the check boxes to toggle on directions; type the
   measurement directions in the text box.

   If you select To Line, distance is relative to the top
   edge of the page. If you select To Position, distance is
   measured from the left edge of the page.

3. Check the settings; then select OK to advance the
   text or graphics to the new position.

## *Notes*

Advance enables you to place the text in relation to the
edges of the page rather than in relation to the margins.
This feature is particularly useful for placing graphics or
text boxes on a page.

By default, WordPerfect sets paper size at 8 1/2-by-
11 inches with a top setting of 1 inch and side margins
of 1 inch.

# Append

### Purpose

Adds new text to the clipboard without deleting the current clipboard contents. Appended text is added to the end of the current data in the clipboard.

### Reminder

The Append option is not available when the clipboard data is a rectangular block or a tabular column. In other words, you cannot append a rectangular block to a rectangular block or a tabular column to a tabular column on the clipboard.

### To append new text to the clipboard

1. Select the text to be appended.
2. Select Edit, Append.

# Auto Code Placement

### Purpose

Inserts codes automatically at the beginning of a page, paragraph, or document (if you are on page one when you insert the code), depending on the codes selected.

### *To turn on Auto Code Placement*

1. Select File, Preferences, Environment.

   The Environment dialog box appears. You see
   `Auto Code Placement` at the top left corner.

2. Select Auto Code Placement to turn on the option.

   A check mark appears in the box next to `Auto Code`
   `Placement` to indicate that the option is turned on.
   To turn off Auto Code Placement, click the check
   mark again.

3. Select OK to save the setting.

### *Notes*

WordPerfect ships with Auto Code Placement turned on.
This default offers automatic code placement at the
beginning of a page or a paragraph.

If the new code is a page code, Auto Code Placement
moves the code to the beginning of the page.

With Auto Code Placement turned off, the new code
takes effect at the location where you inserted it and
affects all text after that point.

# Backup

### *Purpose*

Regularly saves backup copies of files. Timed backups
can protect you from data loss due to power failures by
saving a backup copy of your on-screen document to
disk. Original Document Backup can protect you from
accidental replacement of a document you didn't mean
to replace.

## *To configure Timed Backup*

1. Select File, Preferences, Backup. The Timed Backup dialog box appears.

2. Click the up- or down-triangle symbols next to the Timed Backup text box to increase or decrease the time between backups. You also can press Tab to access the text box, and then type the number of minutes between backups.

3. Select OK or press Enter to save the new settings and return to your document.

## *To turn on Original Document Backup*

1. Select File, Preferences, Backup. The Timed Backup dialog box appears.

2. Click the check box next to Original Document Backup.

   An X appears in the check box to show the option is on.

3. Select OK or press Enter to save the changes and return to the document.

## *Notes*

Timed Backup files are saved in a directory you specify in Preferences, Location of Files. Original Document Backup files are saved in the same directory as your original file, but with a .bk! extension.

By default, Timed Backup is turned on and saves a backup copy of your document every 20 minutes. By default, Original Document Backup is turned off.

# Button Bar

### Purpose

Offers a timesaving way to select commands, features, and options.

WordPerfect ships with a default Button Bar, but you can customize the Button Bar with buttons for your most frequently used commands. You can even create new Button Bars.

To use Button Bars, you must have a mouse.

### To display the default Button Bar

Select View, Button Bar. This procedure works as a toggle. Select View, Button Bar again to hide the Button Bar.

### To create a Button Bar

1. Select View, Button Bar Setup, New. The Edit Button Bar dialog box appears.

2. Click the menu item that you want to add to the Button Bar. The menu item is now a button on the Button Bar.

3. Select OK when you finish configuring the Button Bar. The Button Bar Save dialog box appears.

4. In the Filename text box, type a file name for the Button Bar; then select Save or press Enter to save the Button Bar.

   The Button Bar Save dialog box closes and you return to the Button Bar Edit dialog box.

5. Select OK.

## To reposition the Button Bar on-screen

1. Select View, Button Bar Setup, Options. The Button Bar Options dialog box appears.

2. Select the position that you want for the Button Bar by clicking the circle next to the position.

   These circles are similar to check boxes, except that selected items have a filled circle, not an X. Selecting a new position automatically deselects an old position.

3. Select OK to confirm your choice.

## To change the style of the buttons

1. Select View, Button Bar Setup, Options.

2. In the Button Bar Options dialog box, select style options by clicking the circle next to the option.

3. Select OK or press Enter to confirm and save the changes.

## To change a macro into a button

1. Select View, Button Bar Setup, Edit. The Edit dialog box opens.

2. Click Assign Macro to Button.

   The Assign Macro to Button dialog box appears with a list of macros that are contained in the macro directory. You can select from these macros.

3. Select your choice of a macro.

4. Click Assign. You also can press Alt+A, Enter.

   The macro is assigned to a new button, which is placed on the Button Bar. You return to the Edit Button Bar dialog box.

5. Select OK to save the changes and return to the document.

### *To delete a button*

Drag the button below the Button Bar.

# Cancel, Undelete, Undo

### *Purpose*

Cancels, undoes, or undeletes whatever you just did in
your document.

Cancel cancels the most recent action in your document.
For example, you can use it to back out of a dialog box
without making a selection. Undo reverses the most
recent change you have made to your document.
Undelete restores up to three of the most recent deletions
you have made.

### *To cancel the most recent action*

Press Esc.

### *To use Undo*

Select Edit, Undo or press Alt+Backspace.

The most recent editing change you made to your
document is reversed. If you accidentally deleted a
portion of text, for example, Undo restores the text.

### *To undelete text*

1. Select Edit, Undelete or press Alt+Shift+Backspace.
   The Undelete dialog box opens.

2. Select Restore to insert and highlight the most recent
   deletion. The Undelete dialog box closes and the text
   is restored.

If you are satisfied with the insertion of this text, click anywhere in the document to turn off the highlighting. Otherwise, proceed with step 3.

3. Open the Undelete dialog box again and select Next to see the next deletion or Previous to see the previous deletion. These deletions appear highlighted in the text, and the Undelete dialog box remains open.

4. When the deletion you want to restore is highlighted, select Restore.

# Clipboard

### Purpose

Acts as a temporary holding place where you can store data that you want to pass from document to document or from application to application.

The clipboard is a Windows feature that WordPerfect can use. This feature can save you much additional typing and formatting. You do not see a Clipboard item on any of the menus, but it is available behind the scenes.

### Available clipboard functions

You can perform the following functions with the clipboard:

| Option | Function |
|---|---|
| Cut (Shift+Del) | Cuts Selected text or graphics from a document. The data disappears from the screen but is stored on the clipboard. |
| Copy (Ctrl+Ins) | Copies Selected text or graphics from a document; the data remains in your document, but a copy is also stored on the clipboard. |

| *Option* | *Function* |
|---|---|
| Paste (**Shift+Ins**) | Pastes clipboard contents into your document at the insertion point. |
| Append (**Alt+E,D**) | Appends new selected text to the text already on the clipboard. The new data is added at the end of the old data. |

### Notes

For more detailed instructions on the clipboard commands, look under the listing for each command.

See also *Append*, *Copy*, *Cut*, and *Paste*.

## ═ Close

### Purpose

Closes documents, dialog boxes, and windows. If you have a document open on-screen, this command closes the document and clears the screen.

### To close a document

You can close a document using the following methods:

- Click the Close button on the Button Bar.
- Select File, Close.
- Press **Ctrl+F4**.

### *To close dialog boxes*

Closing a dialog box depends on the particular dialog box, but most have a Close button and a Save button or an OK button. You can close dialog boxes using the following methods:

- Click the small button that looks like the handle of a file drawer at the top left corner of the dialog box.

- If you want to close a dialog box that does not contain a Save, Save As, or OK button, click the Close button. Some dialog boxes, such as the Edit Initial Codes dialog box, save any changes that you have made when you select Close.

- If the dialog box contains a Save, Save As, or OK button, click one of these buttons to save any changes that you made to the dialog box. Then click Close if the dialog box doesn't close itself.

- If you want to insert into your document any codes, styles, or other items that you have specified in the dialog box, click the Insert button.

- If you want to disregard changes that you made to the dialog box, click the Cancel button or press Esc.

### *To close a window*

You can close windows using the following procedures:

- Click the small button that looks like the handle of a file drawer at the top left corner of the window.

- Select Close from the File pull-down menu.

# Columns

### *Purpose*

Makes creating columns a snap!

## *Newspaper columns*

Newspaper columns read from top to bottom; text flows from the bottom of one column to the top of the next.

---

### *To set up newspaper columns*

1. Position the insertion point where you want the columns to begin. Generally, you want the starting point to be at the beginning of the document.

2. Select Layout, Columns or press Alt+L,C. Pressing Alt+L,C opens the Columns menu also. To open the Columns Define dialog box, you can press Alt+L,C,D.

3. Select Define. The Columns Define dialog box opens.

4. Columns On and Evenly Spaced Columns are on by default when you open the dialog box. You must deselect them to turn them off.

5. When the settings are the way you want them, click OK to save settings, start columns at the insertion point, and close the dialog box to return to the document.

## *Parallel columns*

Parallel columns place text side by side, grouped across the page in rows.

---

### *To set up parallel columns*

1. Position the insertion point where you want the columns to begin.

2. Select Layout, Columns or press Alt+L,C to open the Columns menu. To open the Columns Define dialog box, you can press Alt+L,C,D.

3. Select Define. The Columns Define dialog box opens.

4. Columns On and Evenly Spaced Columns are on by default when you open the dialog box. You must deselect them to turn them off.

5. When the settings are the way you want them, click **OK** to save settings and start columns at the insertion point. The dialog box closes and you return to your document.

### *To type text in parallel columns*

1. Position the insertion point in the first column and type the text for that row.

2. Reposition the insertion point in the next column, or press **Ctrl+Enter** to move to the next column. Then type text in that column.

## *Parallel columns with Block Protect*

Parallel columns with block-protect are similar to parallel columns, except that each row of block-protected columns stays together on the page. If one column in a row is long enough to move past a page break, the entire row of columns moves to a new page.

### *To use parallel columns with block protect*

1. Position the insertion point where you want columns to begin.

2. Select Layout, Columns or press **Alt+L, C**. Pressing **Alt+L, C** opens the Columns menu also. To open the Columns Define dialog box, you can press **Alt+L, C, D.**

3. Select Define.

4. Under Column Type, select Parallel Block Protect columns.

5. Check the default settings. Change any settings that you want to change.

6. When the settings are as you want them, click **OK**.

7. Select **OK** to confirm your choice. The dialog box closes and you return to the document.

# Convert

### Purpose

Converts file formats to and from other programs so that you can exchange files with those programs.

### To convert file formats

1. From the File menu, select Open or press F4.

2. Enter the name of the file you want to open.

   If the file is not already formatted for WordPerfect, a Convert File Format dialog box appears.

3. Check the text box to make certain that the format from which you are converting appears correctly. If it doesn't, select the proper format from the pop-up list. You access the pop-up list by clicking the up or down arrow next to the text box. Click the correct format once to highlight it.

   You can use ↑ or ↓ also to scroll through the list by using the keyboard. The fastest way is to type the first letter of the file format you want and then use ↑ or ↓ to get to other formats starting with the same letter, if the first one to appear is not the one you want.

4. Select OK to start the conversion process.

### Note

WordPerfect file format is fully compatible with the WordPerfect 5.1 file format. To save in another format, see *Save As*.

# Copy

### Purpose

Copies selected text to the clipboard without removing it from your document. Later, you can paste a copy of the clipboard contents to any other place in your document or to another document.

### To copy data to the clipboard

1. Select the text you want to copy to the clipboard.

2. Select Edit, Copy or press **Ctrl+Ins**.

   The selected text is copied to the clipboard, but it is not removed from your document.

### To paste data from the clipboard to the document

1. Position the insertion point in the document where you want to copy the clipboard data.

2. Select Edit, Paste or press **Shift+Ins**.

### Notes

You can paste clipboard contents into your document as often as you want until you cut or copy new text. That new text then replaces the clipboard contents.

If you want to copy selected text to another document, you must use Cut rather than Copy to place the text on the clipboard. You can, however, cut the selected text to place it on the clipboard and then immediately select Paste to restore the text to the document.

See also *Cut* and *Paste*.

# Cross-References

## Purpose

References a related topic in another part of a book or other lengthy document.

WordPerfect inserts codes into your document to mark the reference and the target. The reference is where you direct the reader to look in another part of the document for information. The target is the information to which you are directing the reader.

When you later add more references, regenerate the cross-reference. WordPerfect automatically renumbers the references.

## To mark both reference and target

1. Position the insertion point where you want to create a reference.

2. Type introductory text for the cross reference, such as **See page #.**

3. Press the **space bar** to add a space between the introductory text and the page number or other reference type number.

4. Select Tool, Mark Text, Cross-Reference, or press **F12** and select Cross-Reference. The Mark Cross-Reference dialog box appears.

5. Select the Both Reference and Target option.

   A black circle appears in the circle to show that the option is turned on.

6. Select a reference type from the Tie Reference to Target pop-up list.

   You can select Page Number, Paragraph/Outline, Footnote Number, Endnote Number, Figure, Table Box, Text Box, User Box, or Equation Box.

7. Type a unique name in the Target Name text box. WordPerfect will use this name to tie the reference to the target when you generate the cross-reference.

8. Select **OK**.

9. Move the insertion point to the position immediately following the target; then press **Enter**.

   The reference and target codes are inserted and the page number or other tie reference type appears at the reference marker.

10. Repeat steps 1 through 9 for each reference and target in your document.

### *To generate cross-references*

1. Select Tools, Generate or press **Alt+F12**.

2. In the Generate dialog box, select Yes to update all references in the document.

### *Note*

If you reference graphics box numbers, WordPerfect inserts the Caption Number style at each reference code. When you reference page numbers, WordPerfect inserts the Page Number style. If either of these styles includes text, that text appears when you generate the cross-reference.

# Cut

### *Purpose*

Enables you to cut text from a document and store it on the clipboard so that you can paste it into another part of the document, a different document, or another Windows application program.

### *To cut text*

1. Select the portion of text you want to cut.

2. Select Edit, Cut or press Shift+Del to cut the text.

   The selected text is now on the clipboard, ready to paste into another part of your document or into another document.

### *Notes*

You can copy clipboard contents to your document as many times as you want until you cut or copy new text to replace the clipboard contents.

See also *Paste* and *Select*.

# Date and Time Codes

### *Purpose*

Enables you to insert the date and/or time into your document automatically. WordPerfect uses the computer's clock to insert the current date as text into a document.

### *Reminder*

For the Date and Time Codes feature to work properly, the internal clock in your computer must be set to the correct date and time.

### *To insert date codes and/or time codes*

1. Position the insertion point in the document where you want the date to appear.

2. Select Tools, Date, Code or press **Ctrl+Shift+F5**. A date code is inserted into your document. If you have set up time codes, they also appear when you select Tools, Date, Code.

The default date code appears as Month Day, Year. If you prefer for it to appear in abbreviated form or as numbers separated by slashes (/), you must edit the codes in the Date Format dialog box.

### *To change the way the date appears*

1. Select File, Preferences, Date Format. The Date/Time Preferences dialog box opens.

2. Select one of the predefined date codes by clicking Predefined Dates while holding down the left mouse button. Move the mouse to highlight the format that you want from the list; then release the mouse button.

3. Select **OK** or press **Enter** to accept the date code format. WordPerfect uses this format until you change it again.

### *To set up a time code*

1. Select Tools, Date, Format. The Document/Date Format dialog box opens.

2. Click Time Codes and hold down the left mouse button to highlight the codes that you want from the pop-up list.

3. Select **OK**.

The time codes that you select are in effect until you edit the codes in the Date Format dialog box.

### *To edit codes in the Date Format dialog box*

1. Select Tools, Date, Format. The Document/Date Format dialog box opens.

2. Select codes from the pop-up list of predefined codes. You also can customize the format by selecting codes from the pop-up lists on the Date Codes and Time Codes buttons.

   Click the appropriate button and hold down the mouse button to highlight your choice.

   WordPerfect inserts codes into the text box from left to right with no spaces or punctuation between codes.

3. Look at the Date Preview section of the dialog box to preview how the date and time codes will appear in the document.

4. Using the keyboard, add text and punctuation to the codes in the text box.

5. Edit any unwanted codes by selecting them and pressing **Del**.

---

*Notes*

Date and Time Codes can save you time typing and editing. Suppose, for example, that you are sending a form letter on several different days. Rather than enter and reenter the date that you send the letter, you could use Date Codes to insert the current date automatically.

You cannot type numbers, percentage signs (%) or dollar signs ($) in the text box portion of the Date Format dialog box. Instead, you must edit the codes.

If you are using a Language Module, you must change date and time codes by editing the Language Resource File rather than using the Date Format dialog box.

You can add a Date/Time code to a primary merge file. When you run the merge, the date appears in the document automatically.

# Document Comments

## *Purpose*

Inserts comments into your document. The comments
are hidden unless you decide to display them or convert
them to text. You can print comments after you convert
them to text.

## *To insert comments*

1. Position the insertion point where you want the
   comment to appear in the text.

2. Select Tools, Comment, Create. The Create
   Comment dialog box appears.

3. When the Create Comment dialog box opens, the
   insertion point is in the edit-screen portion, and you
   can just type your comment. You can select Bold,
   Underline, or Italic buttons to enhance the text of
   your comment either before or after typing the text.

4. Select OK to save the comment.

5. From the View menu, select Comments to display the
   comment on-screen.

## *To turn a comment into text*

1. Position the insertion point just after the comment
   that you want to convert.

2. Select Tools, Comment, Convert to Text. The
   comment now appears in your document as normal
   text.

# Document Compare

### Purpose

Enables you to compare two versions of the same document.

### Caution!

Save a backup copy of the current document with a distinctive file name before you begin making comparisons. You then have the original file in case you decide against the editing changes.

### To compare two documents

1. Open the first file that you want to compare. You open a file by selecting File, Open or pressing F4. Then highlight the appropriate file.

2. Select Open or press Enter.

3. Select Tools, Document Compare.

4. Select Add Markings. The Add Markings dialog box appears.

5. Type the names of the files you are comparing. If you saved a backup copy of the new file just before comparing, the file name appears in the text box as the default file. You can type the name of a different document to compare in the text box.

6. Select the Compare button. The document on-screen appears with inserted text marked as redline text and deleted text marked as strikeout text.

### To remove markings

1. Select Tools, Document Compare, Remove Markings. The Remove Markings dialog box appears.

2. Select Leave Redline Marks if you want to retain the inserted text marked with redline in your document. If you also want to delete the redline marks, don't select this option.

3. Select **OK** to remove markings.

___

### Notes

You can select Edit, Undo or press **Alt+Backspace** to remove any document compare text and codes and restore the current document to its precomparison state.

WordPerfect compares differences by phrase, rather than by word. The program uses phrase indicators, such as punctuation marks and codes, and compares the text between those indicators. The comparison involves all text, including footnotes, endnotes and tables. It does not compare text in headers, footers, or graphics boxes.

# Document Layout

___

### Purpose

Enables you to create a professional-looking document. Layout is the arrangement and formatting of the document with font codes, margins, paper size and type, styles, and so on.

___

### Reminder

Before typing text, you should set up the basic layout of the document in Document Initial Codes. The formatting codes then will not clutter the document.

___

### To set up Document Initial Codes

1. Position the insertion point at the beginning of an unmodified document.

2. Select Layout, Document, Initial Codes. The Document Initial Codes dialog box opens.

3. Select Layout, Page, Paper Size to open the Paper Size dialog box. You also can press **Alt+F9** and select Paper Size.

4. Select the paper size and type that you want.

5. Click the Select button.

6. Select Layout, Margins or press **Ctrl+F8**. The Margins dialog box opens.

7. Set margins for Left, Right, Top, and Bottom by typing the settings in the text boxes next to each position.

8. Select **OK** or press **Enter** to accept the new margin settings and return to the Document Initial Codes dialog box.

9. Select Layout, Line, Tab Set, or press **Shift+F9** and select Tab Set. The Tab Set dialog box opens.

10. Set tabs by checking the appropriate check boxes and typing information in the text boxes.

11. Select **OK** or press **Enter** to return to the Document Initial Codes dialog box.

12. Select Font, Font or press **F9**. The Font dialog box opens.

13. Select the font that you want.

14. Select font appearance and size attributes by clicking the check boxes beside the options.

15. Select **OK** or press **Enter** to accept your choices and return to the Document Initial Codes dialog box.

16. Select other options. From the Document Initial Codes dialog box, you can

   - *Turn on Widow/Orphan protection.* Select Layout, Page, Widow/Orphan. You also can press **Alt+F9** and select Widow/Orphan.

   - *Turn on Hyphenation.* Select Layout, Line, Hyphenation. You also can press **Shift+F9** and select Hyphenation.

- *Set the justification.* Select Layout, Justification.
  Select the justification that you want by holding
  down the mouse button and selecting the
  appropriate option. You also can press **Ctrl+L**
  for left justification, **Ctrl+R** for right
  justification, **Ctrl+J** for center justification, or
  **Ctrl+F** for full justification.

17. Select the Close button to save your initial codes and
    return to the document.

# Document Summary

## Purpose

Summarizes certain key information about the
document.

A document summary consists of a descriptive name and
type, the author's name, the typist's name, creation and
latest revision dates, subject, account, keywords to
search for, and an abstract. The descriptive name in a
document summary can be as long as 68 characters. If
you use WordPerfect's FileManager, the descriptive file
names can appear in your Quick List. Descriptive type
enables you to sort your files by categories. The abstract
is a brief summary of the document. You can either type
your abstract or permit WordPerfect to append the first
400 words of your document as the abstract.

If you want to create document summaries for most of
your documents, you should change your settings in the
Document Summary Preferences Dialog box.

### To create a document summary

1. From the Layout menu, select Document, Summary.
   You also can press **Ctrl+Shift+F9** and select
   Summary. The Document Summary dialog box
   opens.

2. In the text boxes, type the information that you want in your document summary.

You can specify information in the following text boxes:

### Reference

| *Text Box* | *Purpose* |
| --- | --- |
| Descriptive Name | The entire name (up to 68 characters) of the document. |
| Descriptive Type | The type of document. |
| Creation Date | The original creation date of the document. |
| Revision Date | The date of the latest revision to the document. |

### Information

| *Text Box* | *Definition* |
| --- | --- |
| Author | The person who wrote the document. |
| Typist | The person who typed the document. |
| Subject | What the document is about. |
| Account | Client name or account number, if applicable, for whom you created the document. |
| Keywords | Words that set this document apart from others. |
| Abstract | The first 400 words of the document if WordPerfect creates this automatically; otherwise, the summary that you type of the document. |

3. Select the appropriate buttons for what you want to do with the document summary. You can select Extract, Save As, Delete, Print, OK, and Cancel.

4. Select **OK** to save the information.

### *To save the document summary with the file*

1. Select Layout, Document, Summary. You also can press **Ctrl+Shift+F9** and select Summary. The Document Summary dialog box opens.

2. Either click the **Save As** button or press **Tab** to move the cursor to the Save As button and then press **Enter** to open the Save Document Summary dialog box. Pressing **F3** opens the Save As dialog box for a regular document, but does not work in the Document Summary dialog box.

3. Type a file name in the Filename text box. Be sure to specify full drive and path information if you are saving to a different drive or directory.

4. Select Save.

   The Overwrite/Append File dialog box appears if the file name that you typed in the Document Summary Save dialog box already exists. In this case, proceed to step 5.

5. From the Overwrite/Append File dialog box, select the appropriate choice. You can select the following:

   | *Option* | *Function* |
   |----------|-----------|
   | Overwrite | Replaces the file with the document summary text. |
   | Append | Adds the summary text to the existing file. |
   | Cancel | Cancels changes to the document summary. You return to the Document Summary Save dialog box. |

6. In the Document Summary Save dialog box, type a new file name in the Filename text box. You also can type the full drive and path information to save the summary to a different drive or directory.

7. Select Save to save the summary to the new file name (or to a different drive or directory if you typed path information).

You also can select Cancel to return to the Document Summary dialog box without saving the document summary.

8. In the document Summary dialog box, select Cancel if you want to ignore changes and return to your document.

---

### To extract a document summary from a file

1. Select Layout, Document, Summary. You also can press Ctrl+Shift+F9 and select Summary. The Document Summary dialog box opens.

2. Select Extract.

3. Select Yes to extract all the document summary information and place it automatically into the appropriate text boxes on the Document Summary dialog box.

   Selecting No cancels the operation.

---

### To change document summary preferences

1. Select File, Preferences, Document Summary. The Document Summary Preferences dialog box appears.

2. Enter the Subject Search Text to use for searching for the subject. The default is RE:, but you can enter a different keyword.

3. In the Default Descriptive Type text box, type a description that fits the type of files you most often create.

4. Select Create Summary on Save/Exit if you want WordPerfect to create a summary every time you save a document.

5. Select OK to save the changes.

---

### Notes

If you use FileManager, the descriptive file names can appear in your Quick List.

If you want to create document summaries for most of your documents, you should change the settings in the Document Summary Preferences Dialog box.

# Draft Mode

### *Purpose*

Offers a colorized display of your document as you work. Draft Mode is a faster way to work if you are dealing with a document that has many font changes, graphics, or columns. Characters display monospaced, like those in WordPerfect 5.1.

To make editing easier in Draft Mode, you can assign different colors to elements, such as codes, fonts, subscript, superscript, redlines, strikeout, and so on.

### *To turn on Draft Mode*

Select View, Draft Mode. Select the option again to turn it off.

### *To alter color settings*

1. Select File, Preferences, Display. The Display Settings dialog box appears.

2. Select Draft Mode Colors.

3. Select the Color Settings button at the top of the dialog box. Hold down the left mouse button and move the mouse to highlight a color setting.

   The Color Settings Button pop-up list enables you to select from several predefined color settings.

4. Select OK to set the new colors.

### *To customize color settings*

1. Select File, Preferences, Display. The Display Settings dialog box appears.

2. Select Draft Mode Colors.

3. Click the check box of any appearance or size attribute that you want to recolor.

4. Select your color choice from the foreground and background color palettes.

5. Select OK to accept the changes.

### *Note*

Select Reset and OK to restore the original colors.

# Enhancing Text

### *Purpose*

Improves the look of your document by enabling you to select different font attributes. You also can change font size attributes to make the text appear larger or smaller. Appearance attributes, such as bold and italics, enable you to emphasize important text.

Changing a font at the Font menu changes the font temporarily. To change a font permanently, set up a new initial font.

### *To choose an initial font*

1. Select File, Select Printer. The Printer Select dialog box appears.

2. Select Printer Setup. The Printer Setup dialog box appears.

3. Select Current Initial Font. The Printer Initial Font dialog box appears.

4. Select a font from the font list. You can either click the font to highlight it, or press ↑ or ↓ to highlight your choice.

5. Select **OK** or press **Enter** to accept your choice and return to the Printer Setup Dialog box.

6. From the Printer Setup box, select **OK** to accept your choices and close the Printer Setup box.

   In the Printer Select dialog box, you must select the Update button to update your printer definition with the new initial font and then select the Select button to save the new setting. Selecting Close (or pressing Esc) does not save the new settings but rather cancels any changes you made in Printer Select or Printer Setup.

   The new initial font shows up in any new document you open or retrieve. If you already have a document on-screen in a different font, however, the font does not change.

7. Select Close or press **Esc** to return to your document without saving changes.

### To select text to be enhanced

1. Position the insertion point at the beginning of the text you want to enhance.

2. Press and hold down the left mouse button; then move the mouse to highlight the text you want to include.

3. Release the mouse button.

### To select font attributes from the Font menu

1. From the menu bar, select Font.

2. Select font options by clicking them with the mouse. Select these options again to turn them off.

3. Select Size to pull down a menu of font size options. You can select these options by clicking them.

   The selected text is now enhanced with whatever attributes you chose from the Font menu. Text after the selected text is not affected by the enhancement.

### *To enhance text you are about to type*

1. Select the font attribute that you want to apply.

2. Type the text you want enhanced.

3. Select the attribute again to turn it off when you finish typing the text you want to enhance.

### *To select font appearance attributes in the Font dialog box*

1. Select the text to be enhanced.

2. Select Font, Font or press F9. The Font dialog box opens.

3. Click the check box of the appearance attribute you want to apply to the selected text.

   An X in the check box shows that an option is turned on.

4. Select OK to save changes and return to the document.

5. When you finish selecting enhancements, click the insertion point anywhere in the document to turn off the highlighting for the selected text.

### *To change font size from the Font dialog box*

1. Select Font, Font or press F9. The Font dialog box opens.

2. Click the check box of the size attribute that you want to use.

   An X appears in the check box to show that size is turned on.

3. Preview the size selection by looking at the small box underneath the Font list box. When you change font sizes, the sample sentence in this box changes to show the new size.

4. Select **OK** to put your changes into effect and return to your document.

### *To change the font*

1. Select the text to be enhanced.

2. Select Font, Font or press **F9** to open the Font dialog box.

3. From the Font list box, select the font you want to use.

4. Select **OK** to confirm your selection and return to the document.

### *Font enhancement keyboard shortcuts*

You can use the following keyboard shortcuts to select font enhancements:

| *Key(s)* | *Function* |
|---|---|
| **F9** | Font Menu |
| **Ctrl+N** | Normal Text |
| **Ctrl+B** | Bold Text |
| **Ctrl+I** | Italics |
| **Ctrl+U** | Underline |
| **Ctrl+S** | Opens the Size menu |
| **Ctrl+W** | WP Characters |

## Notes

If you are in the middle of a document when you change the initial font, the document retains the font that you were using when you began typing unless you change it at the Font dialog box. When you begin a new document, the new initial font appears on the status line at the bottom left corner of the screen.

The fonts available in the Font list depend on what printer driver you are using, the capabilities of your printer, and whether or not you installed a print cartridge or a font package, such as Adobe Type Manager, Facelift, or MoreFonts.

# Equation Editor

## Purpose

Enables you to create scientific or mathematical equations.

## To create an equation

1. Select Graphics, Equation, Create. The Editor opens.

2. Create the equation in the editing pane. You can select special symbols and keywords from the Equation Palette.

3. Select Redisplay to view the equation in the display pane.

4. Select Close to save the equation and return to your document.

## To edit an equation

1. Select Graphics, Equation, Edit.

2. In the Equation Editor text box, type the number of the box you want to edit.

3. Select **OK** to confirm your choice.

4. Edit the equation using the following methods:

   - Select Undo to undo the most recent change to the equation.

   - Cut selected text and graphic characters to place them in the clipboard.

   - Paste clipboard contents into the editing pane at the insertion point.

   - Select Settings to open the Equation Settings dialog box and change settings.

5. Select **OK** to confirm your choices.

6. Close the box to return to your document.

---

*Note*

Each equation is given a number when you create it. You must know the equation number to edit the equation later.

# FileManager

---

*Purpose*

Handles such routine file and graphics maintenance chores as copying, moving, and deleting files.

---

*To open FileManager*

Select File, FileManager.

## *FileManager Help*

FileManager Helps explains all the different
FileManager functions and how to use them.

### *To use Help*

1. Click Help at the top right of the FileManager
   window or press **Alt+H**. Help's pull-down menu
   appears with Index highlighted at the top.

2. Select Index with the mouse or press **Enter**.

3. Use the scroll bar to browse through Index and look
   at available Help topics.

### *To search for a topic*

1. Click the Search button or press **Alt+S** to activate the
   Search button. The Search dialog box appears.

2. Type the topic name in the Search For text box.
   WordPerfect displays a list of related topics that you
   can select.

3. From the list, double-click the topic that you want.
   You also can press **Tab** to move to the list and then
   use ↑ and ↓ to highlight the topic, and then press
   **Enter** to select it. Another list of topics appears in the
   Topic(s) Found list box directly below the first list
   box.

4. Use the same techniques in step 3 to select the topic
   you want from the Topic(s) Found list box. You also
   can click the topic with the mouse, and then select the
   Go To button in the Search dialog box.

5. Click the Browse button or press **Alt+R**, **Enter** to
   read related topics.

6. Select File, Print Topic to print a help topic.

7. Select File, Exit to return to FileManager.

# FileManager Navigator

FileManager Navigator shows drive and directory structure and contents and handles file maintenance tasks. From here you can change drives and directories, set up a Quick List or Files List, configure a FileManager Button Bar, or view contents of a selected file in the File View window.

You can use Navigator's File menu to select Preferences in Environment and Associate as startup options. Associate enables you to select other Windows programs to launch from FileManager. Printer Select lets you select your printer, graphics resolution, paper size, landscape or portrait orientation, and initial font.

### To load directory and file lists into File Navigator

1. Select the drive letter of the drive you want to navigate. A list of directories on that drive appears.

2. Select the name of the directory that contains the files you want to access. The list of files for that directory appears.

   You must repeat this step if the directory you want is a subdirectory of the one you just entered.

3. Click the file list of the directory you just entered or press →to make the file list active.

4. Select a file. The Open dialog box appears. Select Open to return to the editing window and open the file. Select Cancel to return to File Navigator.

### To use File Navigator's Viewer

1. Follow steps 1 through 3 in the preceding procedure to see the file list that contains the file you want to view.

2. Select the Viewer to make it active.

3. Select a file name in the file list to display that file in the Viewer.

### To use FileManager Navigator

Use the following procedures within FileManager
Navigator:

- Select options from the File menu of Navigator. You
  also can press **Alt+F** and use ↓ to highlight an option;
  then press **Enter** to select it.

- Change directories by double-clicking a directory
  name in the directory list box. Changing drives works
  the same way—simply double-click the drive letter.

- Use Viewer to view files.

- Select the Search button or press **Alt+S**, **F** to find a
  specific file.

- Select the Word Search button or press **Alt+S**, **W** to
  find a file containing a specific word or phrase.

- Select File, Exit to return to your document when you
  finish using File Navigator.

## Quick List

Quick List, which is user-configurable, provides a list of
the directories you use most often. You can view a list of
directories you have chosen to display in Quick List by
their descriptive names. You select the descriptive
names according to the type of files you keep in each
directory. You also can add and delete directories in
your Quick List with the Quick List Editor.

### To configure Quick List

1. Select View, Edit Quick List. The Edit Quick List
   dialog box appears.

2. Select Add. The Add Item to Quick List dialog box
   opens.

3. In the Directory/Filename text box, type the drive and
   directory that you want to add.

4. In the Descriptive Name text box, type the descriptive
   name you want to use for that directory, if it is
   different from the default name.

5. Select OK or press Enter to save changes and return to the Edit Quick List dialog box.

6. Select OK or press Enter to save your changes, close the Edit Quick List dialog box, and return to File Navigator.

### To delete directories in Quick List

1. Select View, Edit Quick List. The Edit Quick List dialog box appears.

2. Select a directory you want to delete.

3. Select Delete. The Delete item from the list? prompt appears.

4. Select Yes to delete that directory from the list. Select No to leave the directory in the list. You return to the Edit Quick List dialog box.

5. Select OK or press Enter to return to File Navigator. The directories selected for deletion are merely taken out of your Quick List; they are not erased from disk.

### To use Quick List

1. From Navigator's View menu, select Quick List. Your Quick List appears.

2. Select a directory name to display the contents of that directory in the File List dialog box. The File List dialog box appears.

3. Double-click a file to retrieve it. FileManager closes and you return to your document window with the file on-screen.

   You also can use ↓ to highlight the file name and press Enter to select it. The Open dialog box appears. Press Tab until you access the Open button, and then press Enter. FileManager closes and you return to the document with the file open on-screen.

   Select File, Exit to close File List, Quick List, and Navigator without opening a file.

## *File List*

File List displays the contents of a directory, sizes of files, and the date and time the files were last saved.

### *To use the File List*

1. In Navigator, select View, File List. The file list displays the contents of the directory that contains your WordPerfect documents.

2. To change to another directory, type the drive and path information in the text box.

3. Retrieve a file into a document by double-clicking the file.

   You also can use ↓ to highlight the file name, and then press **Enter** to select it. The Open dialog box appears. Press **Tab** until you access the Open Button, and then press **Enter**.

   Select File, Exit to exit File List without retrieving a document.

## *FileManager Button Bars*

This option offers a shortcut way to select the commands, features, and options that you use most often in file management. You must have a mouse to use the Button Bar.

### *To display the Button Bar*

Select View, Button Bar. Select View, Button Bar again to hide the Button Bar.

### *To create a Button Bar*

1. Select View, Button Bar Setup.

2. Select New to open the Edit Button Bar dialog box.

3. Add buttons to the Button Bar by clicking a menu item and dragging the menu item to the Button Bar.

4. Delete a button by clicking it and dragging it off the bar.

### *FileManager shortcut keys*

The following chart includes some function key commands for using FileManager:

| *Key(s)* | *Action* |
|---|---|
| **Ctrl+F** | File List |
| **Ctrl+N** | Navigator |
| **Ctrl+V** | File Viewer |
| **Ctrl+Q** | Quick List |
| **F9** | Font |
| **Shift+F4** | Tile Windows |
| **Shift+F5** | Cascade Windows |
| **Ctrl+F2** | Advanced Find |
| **F2** | Search Active Window |
| **Shift+F2** | Search Next |
| **Alt+F2** | Search Previous |
| **Ctrl+S** | Select All |
| **Ctrl+U** | Unselect All |
| **Ctrl+Ins** | Copy to Clipboard |
| **Alt+Ins** | Append to Clipboard |
| **Ctrl+P** | Print |
| **Ctrl+D** | Delete File |
| **Ctrl+C** | Copy |
| **Ctrl+R** | Move/Rename |
| **Ctrl+A** | Change Attributes |

| Key(s) | Action |
|--------|--------|
| **Ctrl+G** | Change Directory |
| **Ctrl+T** | Create Directory |
| **Alt+F4** | Exit |

### Note

WordPerfect ships with six different default
FileManager View Layouts. These layouts enable you to
determine exactly what you want to see when you open
FileManager. From File Navigator's View menu, select
Layouts; then highlight a layout in the pull-down menu
or select Setup to configure your own.

# Footnotes and Endnotes

### Purpose

Reference material found in the text. Footnotes appear
at the bottom of the page and endnotes are gathered
together at the end of the document or at the ends of
the chapters to which they refer. Text is marked with
numbers, or perhaps an asterisk (*), to indicate that a
footnote or endnote exists for that text.

### To create a footnote or endnote

1. Position the insertion point within the text where you
   want to insert a footnote or endnote number.

2. Select Layout.

3. Select either Footnote or Endnote.

4. Select Options and specify options such as numbering
   style, line spacing, and so on. Select **OK** to save
   settings.

5. Repeat steps 2 and 3, and then select Create.

6. Type the footnote or endnote.

7. Select Close. The note is saved and you return to your document.

### Notes

You can make changes to a footnote or endnote by selecting Layout, Footnote Edit.

To see the footnote or endnote on-screen, turn on Reveal Codes. See *Reveal Codes*.

# Function Keys

### Purpose

Enables you to perform functions quickly by pressing keys or key combinations.

### Available function keys and key combinations

The following list provides the key assignments for the new CUA keyboard:

| Key(s) | Task |
|---|---|
| F1 | Help |
| Shift+F1 | Help-What is |
| Alt+F1 | Thesaurus |
| Alt+Shift+F1 | Unassigned |
| Ctrl+F1 | Speller |
| Ctrl+Shift+F1 | Preferences |

| *Key(s)* | *Task* |
|----------|--------|
| F2 | Search |
| Shift+F2 | Search Next |
| Alt+F2 | Search Previous |
| Alt+Shift+F2 | Unassigned |
| Ctrl+F2 | Replace |
| Ctrl+Shift+F2 | Unassigned |
| F3 | Save As |
| Shift+F3 | Save |
| Alt+F3 | Reveal Codes |
| Alt+Shift+F3 | Ruler |
| Ctrl+F3 | Redisplay |
| Ctrl+Shift+F3 | Draft Mode |
| F4 | Open |
| Shift+F4 | New |
| Alt+F4 | Exit |
| Alt+Shift+F4 | Unassigned |
| Ctrl+F4 | Close |
| Ctrl+Shift+F4 | Clear |
| F5 | Print |
| Shift+F5 | Print Preview |
| Alt+F5 | Paragraph Number |
| Alt+Shift+F5 | Paragraph Define |
| Ctrl+F5 | Date Text |
| Ctrl+Shift+F5 | Date Code |
| F6 | Next Pane |
| Shift+F6 | Previous Pane |
| Alt+F6 | Next Window |
| Alt+Shift+F6 | Previous Window |
| Ctrl+F6 | Next Document |
| Ctrl+Shift+F6 | Previous Document |
| F7 | Indent |
| Shift+F7 | Center |
| Alt+F7 | Flush Right |
| Alt+Shift+F7 | Decimal Tab |
| Ctrl+F7 | Hanging Indent |
| Ctrl+Shift+F7 | Double Indent |

| *Key(s)* | *Task* |
|---|---|
| F8 | Select |
| Shift+F8 | Select Cell |
| Alt+F8 | Styles |
| Alt+Shift+F8 | Special Codes |
| Ctrl+F8 | Margins |
| Ctrl+Shift+F8 | Unassigned |
| F9 | Font |
| Shift+F9 | Line |
| Alt+F9 | Page |
| Alt+Shift+F9 | Columns |
| Ctrl+F9 | Tables |
| Ctrl+Shift+F9 | Document |
| F10 | Menu Bar |
| Shift+F10 | Unassigned |
| Alt+F10 | Play Macro |
| Alt+Shift+F10 | Unassigned |
| Ctrl+F10 | Record Macro |
| Ctrl+Shift+F10 | Stop Macro |
| F11 | Figure Retrieve |
| Shift+F11 | Figure Edit |
| Alt+F11 | Text Box Create |
| Alt+Shift+F11 | Text Box Edit |
| Ctrl+F11 | Horizontal Line |
| Ctrl+Shift+F11 | Vertical Line |
| F12 | Mark Text |
| Shift+F12 | Define lists |
| Alt+F12 | Generate |
| Alt+Shift+F12 | Unassigned |
| Ctrl+F12 | Merge |
| Ctrl+Shift+F12 | Sort |

# Graphics

### Purpose

Offers powerful desktop publishing features by giving you the ability to mix text, type, and graphics from a variety of sources.

### To create a graphics box

1. Position the insertion point where you want to create the box.

2. Select Graphics.

3. Select the type of box.

4. Select Create.

5. In the Create Editor Box, type the text you want in the text box.

6. Close the editor box to save the graphic box and return to your document.

7. Use the mouse to click the graphic and drag it to a new position on-screen.

8. Press the right mouse button to display a menu with options to edit or position the graphics box and its caption.

## Ready-Made Graphics

You can insert ready-made graphics into your document. WordPerfect comes with its own set of graphic figures on disk. These end with a .WPG extension. To use them, you must retrieve them from disk.

### To retrieve a graphic from disk

1. Select Graphics, Figure, Retrieve by clicking with the mouse or pressing F11. The Retrieve Figure dialog box appears.

2. Select View to view the graphics on disk.

3. Select Retrieve to retrieve a graphic figure into your document. You also can double-click the file name.

   Select Cancel to discontinue the retrieval.

4. Reposition the figure on-screen by clicking it with the mouse and dragging it to a new location.

   You also can position the insertion point within the figure and press the right mouse button to bring up the Graphics menu. The Graphics menu enables you to edit or position the graphics box.

## Graphic Lines

WordPerfect enables you to create dramatic vertical and horizontal lines within documents.

### To create graphics lines

1. Select Graphics, Line, Horizontal or Graphics, Line Vertical or press Ctrl+F11 (Horizontal) or Ctrl+Shift+F11 (Vertical).

   The Create Horizontal Line or Create Vertical Line dialog box appears.

2. Set line length and thickness by typing the information in the text boxes under the Line Size heading.

3. Set gray shading by clicking and holding the up- or down-arrow keys next to the Percent text box.

   You can set shading from the keyboard by pressing Tab until you reach the Percent text box, pressing the Backspace key to delete the current information, and typing a new percentage.

4. Click the Position button and highlight your choice of positions.

5. Click OK or press Enter to accept your choices and return to the document.

### *To find and edit graphics lines*

1. Select Graphics, Line.

2. Select Edit Horizontal or Edit Vertical.

   WordPerfect searches backward and then forward from the insertion point until the line is found. The Edit dialog box then opens for that type of line.

3. Make any changes to the line.

4. Click OK or press Enter to confirm your changes.

### *To edit graphics lines with the mouse*

1. Position the insertion point on the line that you want to edit. The insertion point turns into an arrow.

2. Click to select the line

3. Press the right mouse button.

4. An Edit Horizontal or Edit Vertical prompt appears. Either click the prompt or press Enter to open the dialog box appropriate for editing that type of line.

5. From the dialog box that appears, make any changes to the line.

6. Click OK to confirm your changes.

### *Notes*

Horizontal positioning is created as follows:

| *Position* | *Result* |
| --- | --- |
| Left or Right | Positions line against either margin. |
| Center | Centers line between margins. |
| Full | Draws the line from the left edge to the right edge across the page. |
| Specify | Enables you to set the distance from the left edge of the page to the beginning of the line for a vertical |

line or from the top edge of the page for a horizontal line. In the Edit Horizontal Line dialog box, Specify enables you to set the line position in relation to the top edge of the page; in the Edit Vertical Line dialog box, in relation to the left edge of the page.

Vertical positioning is created as follows:

| Position | Result |
| --- | --- |
| Top | Draws the line from the top of the page to the insertion point. |
| Bottom | Draws the line from the bottom of the page to the insertion point. |
| Left Margin | Positions the line to the left of the left margin. |

| Position | Result |
| --- | --- |
| Right Margin | Positions the line to the right of the right margin. |
| Between Columns | Positions the line to the right of the column number that you enter in the text box. |
| Specify | Enables you to position the line a specified distance from the left edge of the page. |

## Line Draw

Line Draw enables you to draw lines in a document using a line-drawing character that you define.

### To use Line Draw

1. Position the insertion point where you want to start drawing lines in the document.

2. Press **Ctrl+D** to open the Line Draw Editing dialog box.

3. Select one of the characters in the Line Draw Characters palette. You can select from 11 predefined characters.

4. From the Modes options, select Draw. This option enables you to draw lines.

5. Use the arrow keys to draw lines and boxes.

   Select Erase mode if you make a mistake or change your mind. You then can use the arrow keys to erase the mistake.

6. Select Move mode to stop drawing or erasing. You then can move the insertion point to a new position on-screen.

7. Select Close to close the Line Draw dialog box and return to your document.

### *To define your own line draw character*

1. Press **Ctrl+D** to open the Line Draw dialog box.

2. Select the Character button. The Line Draw Character dialog box opens.

3. Type the character that you want to use in the text box.

4. Select **OK** or press **Enter** to accept your choice.

### *To use a WP Character in Line Draw*

1. Press **Ctrl+D** to open the Line Draw dialog box.

2. Select the Character button. The Line Draw Character dialog box opens.

3. Press **Ctrl+W**. The WP Characters dialog box opens.

4. Select a character.

5. Select the Insert and Close buttons.

6. Select **OK** or press **Enter** to return to the Line Draw dialog box.

The new WP character is highlighted in the Characters palette.

## Notes

You must use the arrow keys to draw lines in Line Draw. The mouse does not work for drawing, although you can use it to select options in the Line Draw dialog box.

If you want to select from another character set in the WP Characters dialog box, click the Set button while holding down the left mouse button and moving the mouse to highlight your choice. You also can press Tab until you reach the Set button and press the space bar. The list appears, and you can use the arrow keys to highlight your choice.

# Headers and Footers

## Purpose

Places information—such as chapter headings, dates, or the page number—on every page of your printed document. You can have as many as two headers and two footers for each page.

## To create headers and footers

1. Select Layout, Page or press Alt+F9.

2. Select Header or Footer.

3. From the dialog box, select A or B.

4. Select whether to display the header or footer on every page.

5. Select Create to write your header or footer.

6. Select Close to save the header or footer, insert it into your document, and return to the document.

# Help

### *Purpose*

Offers on-line, context-sensitive help for topics and commands that you can access while working in a document. Using Help enables you to learn both basic and advanced WordPerfect functions.

### *Help menu sections*

The Help menu is divided into the following sections:

- Index with Search feature enables you to search for any topic.

- Keyboard (templates and function keys) enables you to learn the new keyboard commands.

- Glossary with definitions explains terms; hold down the mouse button on any term to read the definition.

- "How Do I" sections provide specific procedures.

- "What Is" sections offer extended help for any menu or dialog box.

### *To use What Is*

1. Press Shift+F1. A question mark insertion point appears.

2. Using the mouse, move the question mark pointer to any menu item on which you want more information.

3. Click the item.

### *To access Help with a mouse*

1. Click Help.

2. From the Help menu, click the section you want.

3. Use the scroll bar to scroll to the topic you want to read.

4. Click any topic underlined in green to read that topic.

5. Use Search to find a topic quickly. Use Browse to read related topics.

6. Click File, Print Topic to print any topic.

7. Click File, Exit to return to your document.

### *To access Help with the keyboard*

1. Press Alt+H to open the Help menu.

2. Use the arrow keys to move to the section you want and press Enter.

3. Press S to activate Search. Type in the Search For text box the name of the topic you want help with, and press Enter. Use ↑ or ↓ to highlight a related topic, and then press Enter to read it.

4. Press Alt+F to open the File menu; then type the underlined letter of the option you want.

5. Press Alt+F, X to close Help and return to your document.

# Hyphenation

### *Purpose*

Automatically inserts a hyphen to break words that extend over the right margin of the page. The remainder of the word wraps to the next line.

### To turn hyphenation on or off temporarily

1. Select Layout, Line or press Shift+F9.

2. Select Hyphenation. The Line Hyphenation dialog box opens.

3. Select Hyphenation On to turn on hyphenation.

   The check box in the dialog box is a toggle switch. To turn hyphenation off, select the option again. A check mark in the check box shows that the option is turned on.

4. Select OK or press Enter to accept the new setting and return to your document.

### To turn on hyphenation permanently

1. Select File, Preferences, Environment.

2. Use the check boxes to toggle features off or on.

3. Select OK or press Enter to confirm your choices.

### To cancel hyphenation

1. Position the insertion point directly before the first letter of a word that you do not want hyphenated.

2. Select Layout, Line, Special Codes. The Special Codes dialog box appears.

3. Select Hyphenation Ignore Word; then select Insert.

   A special code is inserted before the word. WordPerfect will not attempt to hyphenate the word again.

   You also can select Ignore when the Hyphenation dialog pops up to ask whether you want to hyphenate the word. You must have Confirm Hyphenation turned on to use this method.

## The Hyphenation Zone

The Hyphenation Zone determines the length of words selected for hyphenation.

### To reset the Hyphenation Zone

1. Select Layout, Line or press **Shift+F9**.

2. Select Hyphenation. The Line Hyphenation dialog box opens.

3. Type new settings in the text boxes for the left and right hyphenation zones.

4. Select **OK** or press **Enter** to accept the new setting and return to your document.

# Indenting

### Purpose

Moves text in from the left margin to the first tab stop.

### To insert indent codes with the keyboard

Use the following keys to insert indents into your text:

| Key(s) | Result |
|---|---|
| F7 | Indents the whole paragraph one tab stop from the left margin. |
| Ctrl+Shift+F7 | Double-indents the paragraph, moving it two tab stops from the left margin. |
| Ctrl+F7 | Creates a hanging indent in which the first line of the paragraph is flush with the left margin and the rest of the paragraph is indented one tab stop from the left margin. |

| Shift+Tab | Moves the insertion point and text one tab stop to the left of the left margin. |
| Tab | Moves only the first line of text to the first tab stop. The remainder of the paragraph is flush with the left margin. |

### *To insert indent codes with the mouse*

1. Position the insertion point where you want to place an indent code.

2. Select Layout, Paragraph. The Indent menu opens.

3. Click the type of Indent you prefer. The insertion point indents.

   You also can use this menu to select Margin Release (Shift+Tab).

### *Note*

You can turn on Reveal Codes to see your indent codes or to delete them if you make a mistake in placement.

# Index

### *Purpose*

Creates an index for a document; automatically generates page number references.

You can mark text to be indexed or you can create a concordance file. The concordance file automatically searches your document for each occurrence of the word or phrase, and then inserts the correct page numbers in the index.

### To create and use a concordance file

1. Open a blank document.

2. Type an entry for the index and press Enter. Place only one item on each line. Repeat until all items are entered.

3. Select File, Save As to save the concordance file.

4. When you define an index, enter the name of the concordance file.

5. Select OK.

### To create an index with marked text

1. Mark the words or phrases in the document that you want in the index. You mark text by selecting the text and pressing F12. This step opens the Mark Index dialog box. Specify the heading and subheadings by typing them into the text boxes and then select OK.

2. Position the insertion point where you want the index to be located.

3. Select Tools, Define, Index, or press Shift+F12 and select Index. This step opens the Define Index dialog box.

4. Select the numbering format.

5. Click OK or press Enter to confirm your choice.

6. Select Tools, Generate or press Alt+F12. WordPerfect generates the index.

# Justification

### Purpose

Affects how your lines of text are arranged in relation to the left and right margins and the center of the page.

### *To change justification*

1. Select Layout, Justification.

2. Select Left, Right, Full, or Center.

### *Notes*

Left justification aligns text flush with the left margin. Right justification aligns text flush with the right margin. Center justification centers text evenly between the left and right margins. Full justification arranges text between the left and right margins by expanding or contracting the spaces between words.

# Keyboard Selection

### *Purpose*

Enables you to switch keyboard layouts. During installation, you are prompted to select either the default CUA keyboard, which is new, or the DOS WP51 keyboard. You can, however, change your keyboard selection after specifying it during installation. You also can design a custom keyboard layout.

### *To change your keyboard*

1. Select File, Preferences, Keyboard. The Keyboard dialog box appears.

2. Choose Select; then select a keyboard file from the Select Keyboard File dialog box.

3. Choose Select again; then click OK or press Enter to confirm your choice.

### *To edit or create your keyboard layout*

1. Select File, Preferences, Keyboard. The Keyboard dialog box appears.

2. Select Edit or Create. The Keyboard Editor Dialog Box appears, which contains an Items Type list.

3. Select Current Keystrokes. Type the keystrokes you want to assign to an item.

4. If the keystrokes are already assigned to an item, the name and type of item appear in the Current Text Line. If `Unassigned` appears in the Current Text Item, proceed to step 5.

5. Select an item from the Item List Box. The name and type of item appear in the New Text line.

6. Select `OK`, and then select Save to save your new keyboard layout.

7. Type a file name in the Filename text box. Give the keyboard files a .WWK extension so that WordPerfect can find them.

# Labels

### *Purpose*

Enables you to create mailing labels, tickets, and side-by-side landscape pages.

To create labels, you first must set up a labels form for your particular printer. If you have a laser printer, follow the directions for setting up a labels form for sheets of labels. If you are using a dot-matrix or daisywheel printer, skip to the section about setting up a labels form for tractor feed labels.

WordPerfect 5.1 for Windows was shipped with a labels macro that enables you to select a labels definition from a predefined list of Avery labels for either laser or dot-matrix printers.

## *Sheet Labels*

For sheet labels, paper size refers to the size of the entire sheet of labels. Label size refers to the size of the individual labels. You may set margins for both paper size and labels.

Suppose, for example, that you have a sheet of labels that is on 8 1/2-by-11-inch backing. The labels are 3 across and each column contains 10 rows. The individual labels are 3-by-15/16 inches and separated from each other by 1/16 inch. The paper size is 8 1/2-by-11 inches. Leave the label margins at 0-by-0 inches for the moment.

You calculate the page margins by measuring the distance from the top edge of the paper to the place on the first label where you want printing to begin. From the left edge of the paper, measure the distance to where you want printing to begin on the label for the Left Edge measurement.

### *To set up a paper size and type for sheets of labels*

1. Make sure that you have selected a printer.

2. Select Layout, Page, Paper Size. The Paper Size dialog box appears.

3. Select Add. The Add Paper Size dialog box appears.

4. Select Labels as the paper type.

5. Change other options as necessary, such as paper size, orientation, and location. If you are printing an entire sheet of labels, specify the size of the entire sheet as your paper size.

6. Select Labels to open the Edit Labels dialog box.

7. Change the label settings to show the size of the individual labels, margins of the labels, and so on.

8. Select OK to confirm your changes and return to the Add Paper Size dialog box. You should see your labels listed in the paper size window.

9. Select OK again.

10. Start labels by positioning the insertion point where you want labels to begin; then select Layout, Page, Paper Size.

11. Highlight the label form by clicking it; then choose Select.

12. Use Reveal Codes to see the label code inserted into your document.

## Tractor Feed Labels

You should treat each row of labels in tractor feed labels as a separate "sheet" of labels. The number of rows is always 1, and the distance between labels is always 0. Paper size should account for the distance between labels.

To calculate paper size, measure the distance from the top of the first label to the top of the label in the row beneath it. Suppose, for example, that the actual size of the label is 3-by-15/16 inches high, and the labels are 1/16 inch apart; your paper height would be 1 inch.

Treating each row of labels as a single sheet of labels does not alter the specifications you give for label size (or the distance between columns if you are using multiple column labels). You should give these measurements as the actual label size. For single-wide labels of 3-by-15/16 inches, you set up a paper size of 3-by-1 inches, but a label size of 3-by-15/16 inches. Top left measurements for tractor feed labels should be 0-by-0 inches.

### To set up a labels form for tractor feed labels

1. Select Layout, Page, Paper Size. The Paper Size dialog box appears.

2. Select Add.

3. Select Labels as your paper type.

4. Change the paper size to the size of your label plus the distance between labels.

5. Select Labels. The Edit Labels dialog box appears.

6. Type the label size, distance between labels, top left measurements, and other specifications. Check for accuracy; then select OK to confirm your selection.

   You return to the Add Paper Size dialog box.

7. Select OK to return to the document window.

8. Start labels by selecting Layout, Page, Paper Size; highlighting the label form in the list; and choosing Select. Labels are inserted at the current location of the insertion point.

## Other Label Procedures

Use the following procedures to produce your labels.

### To type label text (if you are only creating a few labels)

1. Position the insertion point where you want labels to begin.

2. Start labels by selecting label paper definition for either laser (sheet) or tractor feed labels.

3. Use Reveal Codes to see where to start typing on the first label.

4. Press Enter to end a line of text and move to the next line within the label. Press Ctrl+Enter (Hard Page) to move to the next label immediately after finishing the first one.

5. If your text doesn't fit on the label, try using a smaller font.

6. Select File, Print Preview to check your work before printing.

## Merged Labels

To merge labels, you first set up a secondary file with names and addresses. You then set up a primary file with the fields you want on the mailing label.

### To create a primary file for labels

1. At the beginning of a new document window, select your labels form.

2. Position the insertion point where you want to begin typing.

3. Select Tools, Merge, Field.

4. Enter the field number from the secondary file that you want on the label. Press the space bar once and repeat for the next field. Enter field codes as required, ending each field with **Alt+Enter**.

   Make sure that your field numbers correspond with the field numbers in your secondary file.

5. Save the primary file with a distinctive name.

6. Select Tools, Merge or press **Ctrl+F12**.

7. Select Merge to begin the merge.

8. Select File, Save As to save the merged file. You then can print the labels.

### Notes

Print a few test labels on plain paper to check for print and label alignment before merging the labels. You may need to physically move the paper around in the printer to ensure correct alignment.

See also *Merge* and *Reveal Codes*.

# Line Height

### Purpose

Enables you to alter the appearance of a document by changing line height.

### To change line height

1. Select Layout, Line, Height. The Line Height dialog box appears.

2. Click the Fixed Position check box in the dialog box to change from Auto to Fixed.

3. Click the text box and type the new line height.

4. Select OK to confirm your choice.

# Line Spacing

### Purpose

Adjusts line spacing and line height to improve the appearance of your document.

### To change line spacing

1. Select Layout, Line, Spacing. The Line Spacing dialog box appears.

2. Click the arrow buttons on the right side of the text box until the setting that you want appears in the text box.

3. Select OK to confirm your choice.

# Link DDE

### Purpose

Enables you to link data from other DDE (Dynamic Data Exchange) applications. For example, you can link spreadsheet figures from a Windows spreadsheet to a WordPerfect For Windows document. If you change the figures in your spreadsheet, WordPerfect automatically updates the figures in your document.

### To create a DDE Link

1. Position the insertion point in your document where you want to create a link.

2. Select Edit, Link, Create. The Create DDE Link dialog box appears.

3. Select the appropriate source file name from the list displayed. The name in the text box then appears under Source File and Item.

4. In the Link Name text box, type a name for the link.

5. Select Automatic or Manual mode and choose whether you want data stored as text or graphics in your document.

6. Select OK to insert the link. The box closes and you return to your document.

### Note

If you select Automatic mode, data is updated in your WordPerfect document when you update your source file.

# Lists

### Purpose

Enables you to create a list of keywords or headings in a document. You can create indexes, tables of contents, tables of authorities, lists, and cross-references.

### To create a list

1. Select the text to mark for the first item.

2. Select Tools, Mark Text or press **F12**. Select the type of list you want to create: Index, Table of Contents, Table of Authorities, or List.

3. In the Mark List dialog box, type in necessary information, such as title, list number, numbering style, and so on. Select **OK** to confirm your choice.

4. Continue selecting and marking text for each item; select **OK** after each item to add it to the list.

### To define a list

1. Select Tools, Define. The Define List dialog box appears.

2. Select the correct list type.

3. Select the list number and type by clicking the List button and using the mouse to select your choice.

4. Select the numbering format (or no numbering) by clicking the Numbering Format button and selecting your choice.

5. Select **OK** to confirm your choice.

### To generate a list

1. Generate the list on a separate page by inserting a hard page break. You insert a hard page break by pressing **Ctrl+End**.

2. On the new page, type the title of the list and press **Enter** several times to insert blank lines between the title and the list.

3. Position the insertion point where you want the list inserted.

4. Select Tools, Generate. The list appears on the new page.

*Notes*

To delete an item from the list, open Reveal Codes and position the insertion point in the list marker by that item. Press **Del**.

WordPerfect enables you to create up to 10 lists per document. List numbers 1-5 are for text. List numbers 6-10 are reserved for captions of figures, tables, text boxes, user boxes, and equations.

If you select predefined lists (numbers 6-10), you do not have to mark the captions. WordPerfect marks the captions for you. You can, however, add text to this list by selecting and marking it.

See also *Reveal Codes*.

# Macros

*Purpose*

Records a sequence of keystrokes that you can play back later.

*To record a macro*

1. Select Macro, Record.

2. In the Macro Name text box, type a file name for the macro.

3. In the Descriptions text box, type a description of the macro.

4. Select Record.

5. From the menus, select the commands you want included in the macro.

6. Select Macro, Stop to stop the macro recording.

### *To play back a macro*

1. Select Macro, Play. The Play Macro dialog box appears.

2. From the file list, select the macro you want to play.

3. Select the Play button.

### *To assign macros to the Macro menu*

1. Select Macro, Assign to Menu. The Assign Macro to Menu dialog box appears.

2. Select Insert. The Insert Macro Menu Item dialog box appears.

3. Type the macro name in the Macro Name text box; then type a brief description of the macro in the Macro Description text box.

4. Click the button on the Macro Name text box to display a files list and select the macro you just specified. The Select File dialog box appears.

5. Highlight the macro and choose the Select button.

6. Select OK to close the Insert Macro Menu box. The macro you just assigned appears in the Assign Macro to Menu box.

7. Select OK again. You now can select the macro from the Macro menu whenever you want to use it.

# Margins

### *Purpose*

Determines how text is placed on the page. You can set the top, bottom, left, and right margins. The default margins are one inch around the entire page.

### *To set margins from the dialog box*

1. Position the insertion point where you want the margin change to take place.

2. Select Layout, Margins or press Ctrl+F8.

3. Type new margin settings in the dialog box.

4. Select OK to confirm your choice. The change takes effect at the insertion point and stays in place until you change margin settings.

### *To set margins from the Ruler*

1. Select View, Ruler or press Alt+Shift+F3.

2. Position the insertion point where you want the new tab settings to take effect.

3. Use the following techniques when creating and editing tabs:

   • Click a tab marker on the Ruler and drag it to the new position. Release the mouse button when the marker is in place.

   • Delete a tab by selecting it and dragging it below the Ruler.

   • Add a tab by dragging one of the tab markers to any position on the Ruler.

   • Change a tab to a dot leader tab by pressing the button next to the tab pictures on the Ruler to display the dot-leader tab markers; then dragging a tab marker to the Ruler.

# Master Document

### *Purpose*

Organizes large writing projects into a fixed format used for generating indexes, tables of contents, and automatic page numbering while still enabling you to work on individual subdocuments.

A master document contains codes linking the master to all the subdocuments that go with it.

### *To use a master document to organize large projects*

1. Create the subdocuments and store them as individual files.

2. Create the master document and insert subdocument links to show WordPerfect where the subdocuments should be located within the master document. Make sure that you insert the subdocument links in the correct order.

3. Expand the master document to pull in all the subdocuments.

4. Generate the index and table of contents.

5. Condense the master document and store the subdocuments as individual files again.

### *To create the master document and insert subdocument links*

1. Start the master document on a clear screen.

2. Position your insertion point where you want to insert the link.

3. Select Tools, Master Document, Subdocument.

4. Type the file name or select a file; then select OK.

5. Repeat step 4 until all subdocument links are entered.

6. Select Tools, Master Document, Expand Master to expand the master document and pull in all the sublinks.

### *Notes*

If you want each of your subdocuments to start on a fresh page, press Ctrl+Enter to place a hard page break after each entry in the master document.

You must expand the Master Document before you can create and generate an index or table of contents.

Condensing a master document removes the subdocuments from the master document and stores them as separate files, but the links remain intact.

To condense a master document, select Tools, Master Document, Condense Master.

# Math

### Purpose

Calculates simple math formulas with the Tables feature. You can define formulas to add, subtract, multiply, and divide numbers; then enter those formulas into the cells of this minispreadsheet table.

### To use Table Math

1. Position the insertion point in the cell where you want the results of the calculation to appear.

2. Select Layout, Tables, Formula, or press Ctrl+F9 and select Formula.

3. Enter a formula in the text box.

4. Select OK to confirm your choice.

5. Type the numerical values for the cells your formula references in their respective cells.

6. Make sure that the insertion point is inside the table.

7. Select Calculate.

### To copy a formula to another cell

1. Position the insertion point in the cell containing the formula you want to copy.

2. Select, Layout, Tables, Formula, or press **Ctrl+F9** and select Formula.

3. In the To Cell text box, type the cell address to which you want to copy the formula. You also can select Down or Right; then type the number of times you want to copy the formula to the cells to the right of the formula or to the cells below it.

4. Select **OK** to confirm your choice.

# Merge

### *Purpose*

Combines two files into one file, inserting variable data into a fixed format as you run the merge.

You must create two files to merge—the secondary file and the primary file. The secondary file contains the information (such as names and addresses) that you will merge into the primary file. Each field number in the primary file corresponds to a field number in the secondary file.

If you are doing a very long merge, you might prefer to send the merge directly to the printer. If so, you must insert Merge Codes at the end of your primary file.

### *To create a secondary file*

1. Type the first field of information in the document. For example, the first field might be a title (such as **Mr.**, **Mrs.**, or **Dr.**).

2. Press **Alt+Enter** immediately after you enter the first field. Do not leave a space. `Field #1` appears in your document.

3. Continue typing the fields of the first record, remembering to press **Alt+Enter** at the end of every field.

For a form letter you may want to have fields for title, first name, last name, street address, city, state and ZIP code, and salutation. Each of these fields is numbered consecutively, so plan ahead in creating your fields.

4. Press **Alt+Shift+Enter** to end the record. This key combination inserts an [HPg] code in the document and places the insertion point at the beginning of the next record.

5. Continue typing records until you have your entire mailing list in the secondary file.

6. Save the secondary file with a distinctive name. For a Christmas letter address list, for example, you might choose **XMAS.SF**.

### *To create a primary file*

1. Set up the format you want to use for your letter, such as margins, line spacing, font, and so on.

2. Type any text, such as the date, that you want to appear before you insert the first field of a record.

3. Position the insertion point where the first field is to start.

4. Select Tools, Merge, Field, or press **Ctrl+F12** and select Field. The Insert Merge Code dialog box appears.

5. Type the number of the field you want to insert. Suppose, for example, that field #1 is the title (**Mr.**, **Mrs.**, **Dr.**) of the person you are writing. You would type **1** in the Insert Merge Code dialog box. A code such as 1~ appears in your document.

6. Continue inserting fields at the appropriate places in your document by repeating steps 1 through 5 until you have entered all the fields. Add proper spacing and punctuation where needed.

7. Type the text of the letter.

8. Save the letter with a distinctive file name. For example, save a Christmas letter to clients with a file name like **XMAS.PF**.

### *To merge primary and secondary files*

1. Select Tools, Merge, Merge by clicking with the mouse or pressing **Ctrl+F12, M**. The Merge dialog box appears.

2. Type the names of your primary and secondary files in the appropriate text boxes.

3. Select **OK** to confirm your choice. The two files merge on-screen.

4. Save your merged list with a distinctive name. For example, if your document is a Christmas greetings letter, save it as **XMAS.LTR**.

### *To insert merge codes to merge at the printer*

1. Position the insertion point at the end of your primary file on a blank line.

2. Select Tools, Merge, Page Off to insert the Page Off code into the primary file.

3. Select Tools, Merge, Merge Codes to open the Insert Merge Codes dialog box.

4. Scroll down the list of commands in the dialog box until you see {PRINT}. Click to highlight it, and then select Insert to insert it into your document.

5. Close the dialog box to return to your document.

6. Save your file and run the merge. The Page Off and Print codes send your merged letter to the printer.

### *Notes*

You may have as many fields in a record as you like. The individual items (such as first name) are known as *fields*. All the fields that belong together (such as name and address for one person) make up a *record*. You may have as many records as there are names on your address list.

Each data record in a secondary file must have the same number of fields, even if you have to leave one of the fields blank. Each field within within the records must be in the same order.

# Numbering Lines

### Purpose

Numbers lines in your document automatically.
If you move the text around, the numbers are updated automatically to reflect the new positions.

### To number lines

1. Position the insertion point where you want to start numbering lines.

2. Select Layout, Line menu, Numbering. You also can press **Shift+F9** and select Numbering. The Line Numbering dialog box appears.

3. Click the Line Numbering button, hold down the left mouse button, and move the mouse until the highlight is on either `Continuous` or `Restart Each Page` in the menu. Release the mouse button.

4. Select **OK** to save your choice.

### To turn off line numbering

1. Position the insertion point where you want to turn off line numbering.

2. Select Layout, Line, Numbering, or press **Shift+F9** and select Numbering.

3. Click the Line Numbering button, hold down the left mouse button and move the mouse until Off is highlighted. Release the mouse button.

4. Select OK to confirm your selection.

### Notes

You may change line numbering options, such as the position of the line number, the starting number, and whether or not to count blank lines. Simply click the appropriate buttons in the Line Numbering dialog box. You do not see the numbers as you type, but they appear in the printed document. To see how line numbers look before printing, preview the document.

See also *Printer Preview*.

# Numbering Pages

### Purpose

Numbers pages automatically and prints the numbers on the page where you specify to print them.

### To number pages

1. Position the insertion point where you want to start numbering pages. Generally, you begin page numbering at the beginning of the document.

2. Select Layout, Page, Numbering, or press Alt+F9, N. The Page Numbering dialog box opens.

3. Select and specify options by clicking the appropriate buttons while holding down the left mouse button; highlight your choice on the pull-down menus; then release the mouse button. You also can type the required information in the text boxes.

4. Type the number you want to start with in the New Page Number text box. Generally, you will start with 1. You can also select this option to start renumbering pages at any point in your document.

5. In the Accompanying Text box, type any text and punctuation to be printed with the page number.

6. Select Force Current Page Odd to start the page numbering with an odd number. Select Even to start with an even number.

7. Select the position on the page where you want the page number to print.

8. Select Insert Page Number to insert the page number at the position of the insertion point.

9. Select OK to confirm your choice and return to the document.

### *Notes*

Page numbering does not appear on-screen, but will print with your document. To see page numbering, use Print Preview.

See also *Print Preview*.

# Numbering Paragraphs

### *Purpose*

Numbers paragraphs for you in either Auto or Manual mode. Auto mode is defined more rigidly, and WordPerfect calculates the level numbers according to the location of the insertion point when you turn on paragraph numbering. Manual mode enables you to set a fixed level for the paragraph numbers without relation to tab settings.

### To number paragraphs

1. Position the insertion point where you want to start numbering paragraphs.

2. Select Tools, Outline, Paragraph or press **Alt+F5**. The Paragraph Numbering dialog box opens.

3. Select Auto numbering if you want WordPerfect to define the paragraph numbering level for you.

   Select Manual numbering if you want to set a fixed level number; then type a level number in the text box.

4. Select Insert to insert the paragraph number, close the box, and return to your document.

### Notes

To delete the numbering code, turn on Reveal Codes, position the insertion point on the paragraph numbering code, and press **Del**.

See also *Reveal Codes*.

# Open File

### Purpose

Opens a file into the document window and optionally enables you to copy, move/rename, find, or delete a file in the current directory.

### To bring up the Open File dialog box

1. Select File, Open or press **F4**.

2. Double-click the File you want to open. You also can press **Tab** until you access the list of files, use the arrow keys to highlight the file, and press **Enter**.

3. Double-click a directory name if the file that you want is in another directory. You also can press **Tab** until you access the Quick List, press ↓ to highlight the directory, and press **Enter**.

   The list of files contained in the selected directory appears.

4. View a file by clicking the file name to highlight it; then select View. You also can press **Alt+I** or press **Tab** until you access the file list, use the arrow keys to select the file, and press **Alt+V** to view it.

### *To delete files*

1. Highlight the file to delete; then click the Options button while holding down the left mouse button and moving the mouse to highlight the Delete option.

   You also can press **Alt+T**, press the **space bar** to display the Options pop-up menu, use the arrow keys to access Delete, and press **Enter**.

2. From the Delete Files dialog box, select Delete to delete the file or Cancel to cancel the deletion.

### *To copy files*

1. From the files list, select the file that you want to copy.

2. From the Options pop-up menu, select Copy.

3. In the text box, type the new file name, a new path name, or both.

4. Select Copy to copy the file. Select Cancel to cancel the procedure.

### To move or rename files

1. From the files list, select the file that you want to move or rename.

2. From the Options pop-up menu, select Move/Rename.

3. To rename the file, type the new file name in the text box; then select Move.

   To move the file to a new directory, type the full path name of the new directory in the text box; then select Move.

   To rename and move the file, type a new file name and new path name in the text box; then select Move.

### To use the Find option

1. Select the Options button; then select Find from the pop-up list. The Find dialog box appears, and it displays the current directory.

2. Select the Find Files button. The Find Files dialog box appears.

3. In the File Pattern text box, type the name of the file for which you are searching.

4. Select the appropriate button to search the current directory, current subtree, or current drive; then select Find.

   The Find dialog box displays the files that match the file pattern.

### To find files by searching file contents for keywords

1. From the Open File dialog box, select the find option. The Find dialog box opens.

2. Select the Find Words button. The Find Words dialog box appears.

3. Type a word, phrase, or word pattern in the Word Pattern dialog box; then select Find.

The Find dialog box list displays the files that contain the word pattern you specified.

### Notes

You can use wild cards (* and ?) to specify a group of files to delete, copy, move, rename, and so on.

You can use semicolons, spaces, commas, quotation marks, and dashes in word search pattern to define a narrower search. Use a semicolon (;) or space ( ) between two words to find files that contain those two words. The words do not have to appear in consecutive order in the file.

Use a comma (,) between two words to find files using either of the two words, but not necessarily both of them.

Use quotation marks ("") around groups of words to hunt for files containing phrases.

Use a dash (–) to look for files that do not match a pattern after the dash, but that do match the word before the dash.

# Outlines

### Purpose

Create an automatic outline structure upon which you build an outline of your document. If you later move elements of the outline to another position in the document, WordPerfect renumbers them for you.

### *To create an outline*

1. Position the insertion point where you want to start the outline.

2. Select Tools, Outline, Outline On or press **Alt+T, O, O**. Outlining begins at the insertion point.

3. Press **Enter** to automatically insert the first-level paragraph number.

4. Type the text for the first number; then press **Enter** to insert another first-level number.

5. Press **Enter** and then **Tab** to insert a second-level number. Press **Tab** twice for a third-level number.

6. Repeat steps 3 through 5 until you have finished typing the outline.

7. Select Tools, Outline, Outline Off or press **Alt+T, O, F**.

### *To change outline default settings*

1. Select Tools, Outline, Define or press **Alt+Shift+F5**. The Define Paragraph Numbering dialog box opens.

2. Select the paragraph-numbering format by clicking the Predefined Formats button and holding down the left mouse button. Drag the mouse to highlight the format; then release the mouse button.

3. Select a style by clicking the Change button and holding down the left mouse button to highlight a style; then release the mouse button.

4. Select other options by clicking their check boxes. Clicking them again turns them off. Defaults are set so that pressing **Enter** inserts a paragraph number, Auto Adjust to Current Level is set to On, and Attach Previous Level is set to On.

5. Type a new paragraph starting number in the text box to start numbering at a character other than I (the default).

6. Choose OK to close the box and return to the document.

These procedures create a structured outline in which pressing Enter inserts a paragraph number; you can copy entire families of paragraph numbers and accompanying text to a different location in the outline and WordPerfect will renumber them correctly.

You also can make an outline with the paragraph-numbering feature, however. Choose this method to insert a paragraph number anywhere in a document without having to turn Outline on or off and fix paragraph numbers at a specific level and insert them automatically.

### *To use paragraph numbering for outlining*

1. Position the insertion point where you want to start the outline.

2. Select Tools, Outline, Paragraph Number or press Alt+F5. The Paragraph Numbering dialog box opens.

3. Choose Auto or Manual mode.

   In Auto mode, WordPerfect selects the numbering level for you, depending on the settings in the Define Paragraph Numbering dialog box and the location of your insertion point. In Manual mode, you can set the level number without respect to Tab settings.

4. Click the Insert button or press Tab to move the cursor to it and press Enter to insert the first paragraph number at the insertion point. The dialog box closes and the document returns.

### *Note*

You might want to try the outlining and paragraph-numbering features in a blank document first to see how they work and how the various number levels appear.

# Page Breaks

### Purpose

Controls where one page ends and the next begins.

There are two kinds of page breaks—soft and hard. WordPerfect automatically inserts a soft page break, which appears as a dashed line, when you fill one page of text and begin another. If you add or delete text, the page break adjusts accordingly. The hard page break appears as a double line. You insert this page break manually, and it doesn't adjust when you add or delete text in a document.

### To add and delete page breaks

Use these methods to insert and delete page breaks:

- Press **Ctrl+Enter** to end a page and begin a new one. This key combination inserts a hard page break at the location of the insertion point.

- Delete page breaks by opening Reveal Codes. Position the insertion point on the [SPg] or [HPg] code and press **Del**. (See also *Reveal Codes*.)

## Block Protect

Use this feature anytime you want to prevent a block of text from being split in two by a soft page break. The entire block moves to the next page below the page break if it is protected. You can use block protect on text or boxes.

### To protect a block of text

1. Select the block of text.

2. Select Layout, Page, Block Protect, or press **Alt+F9** and select Block Protect.

# Widows and Orphans

A widow is the first line of a paragraph that begins on the last line of a page; an orphan is the last line of a paragraph that begins on the first line of a page. Turning on widow and orphan protection ensures that your document does not contain widows or orphans.

### To turn on widow and orphan protection

1. Position the insertion point where you want protection to begin.

2. Select Layout, Page, Widow/Orphan, or press Alt+F9 and select Widow/Orphan.

### Reminder

From the Files menu, you can go to Preferences, Initial Codes and turn on Widow/Orphan protection permanently. (See *Preferences*.)

# Conditional End of Page

The conditional end of page command keeps a specified number of lines together on a page.

### To turn on conditional end of page

1. Count the lines that you want to keep together on the same page.

2. Position the insertion point at the beginning of the line directly above these lines.

3. Select Layout, Page, Conditional End of Page, or press Alt+F9 and select Conditional End of Page.

4. In the text box, enter the number of lines that should remain together.

5. Select OK.

# Paper Definitions

### *Purpose*

Enables you to select different types and sizes of paper. The types of paper and their sizes are called *paper definitions*. After you set them up, you can switch to them when necessary. You also can add paper definitions to the Paper Size dialog box.

### *Caution!*

If you try to insert a paper size code within columns or tables, an error message appears specifying that the code will not be inserted. If you want to print tables or columns on a different paper size, set up the paper definition before you set up the table or columns, or insert the code before the beginning of the table.

### *To select paper definitions*

1. Make sure that you selected a WordPerfect printer driver rather than a Windows printer driver.

2. Position the insertion point at the location in the document where you want to change paper size or type. If Auto Code Placement is on, you can position the pointer anywhere in the page and the code is inserted at the beginning of the page.

3. Select Layout, Page, Paper Size or press Alt +F9 and select Paper Size. The Paper Size dialog box opens.

4. In the dialog box, highlight the paper definition you want by clicking it. Then click Select to choose the definition and return to your document.

### To add a paper definition

1. In the Paper Size dialog box, select Add to open the Add Paper Size dialog box.

2. In the Add Paper Size dialog box, select paper type by clicking the Paper Type button and holding down the mouse button; then move the mouse to highlight your choice and release the mouse button.

3. Change other options as necessary.

4. Select OK to save the changes and return to the Paper Size dialog box.

5. Highlight the new paper definition in the list by clicking it. Then choose Select to change to the new definition.

# Password Protection

### Purpose

Keeps documents confidential by enabling you to assign a password to them.

### Caution!

Use this feature with caution. If you lose your password, not even WordPerfect can open the file for you again.

### To set or remove a password

1. Open or retrieve the file you want to password protect.

2. Select File, Password.

3. Type the password and select Set. Retype the password for verification and select Set again.

4. Save the document. It is now password protected.

### Notes

Passwords appear on-screen as asterisks. Passwords are not case-sensitive, and they can be up to eight characters long.

To remove a password, open the document, select File, Password, and select Remove.

# Paste

### Purpose

Inserts clipboard data into another part of your document, another document, or another Windows application program.

### To paste clipboard contents into a document

1. Position the insertion point where you want the clipboard contents to appear.

2. Select Edit, Paste or press Shift+Ins.

### To paste data to another document

1. Create or retrieve the file to which you want to paste data.

2. Select File, New or press Shift+F4 to open a new document window.

3. Create or retrieve the file from which you want to select text for pasting.

4. Select the text that you want to paste, and cut or copy it to the clipboard.

5. From the menu bar, select Window. Then select the window with the document you want to paste to.

6. Position the insertion point where you want to paste the clipboard contents.

7. Select Edit, Paste or press Shift+Ins.

### Notes

To have clipboard contents to paste, you must first cut or copy the text.

You can paste clipboard data to another document in another Windows application. Simply open the other application and paste in clipboard contents.

See also *Clipboard*, *Copy*, and *Cut*.

# Preferences

### Purpose

Enables you to customize WordPerfect to suit your needs and preferences.

### To use the Preferences menu

Use the following methods to use the Preferences menu:

- Select File, Preferences; then select an option from the menu.

- Press Ctrl+Shift+F1; then select a menu item.

- Press Alt+F, E; then type the underlined letter in a menu item.

### Available Preference selections

The following list shows the various Preferences
selections:

| Option | Function |
| --- | --- |
| Backup | Sets the timed backup interval for backups. |
| Date Format | Sets Date Text, Date Code, or Date Format and Time Format. |
| Display | Sets display appearance and draft mode color. |
| Document Summary | Sets document summary defaults. |
| Environment | Sets environment defaults, such as Auto Code Placement, Ruler options, Hyphenation options, Prompts, Beep On, and Menu display defaults. |
| Equations | Sets options affecting the display of equations. |
| Initial Codes | Sets format defaults. You can override any of these defaults temporarily in an individual document by selecting new settings from the menu bar. |
| Keyboard | Selects the default keyboard and key assignments. |
| Location of Files | Sets directories where you want WordPerfect to find certain types of files. |

| Option | Function |
|--------|----------|
| *Merge* | Sets up Field and Record Delimiters. |
| Print | Sets print controls, Windows print drivers, and Redline method. |
| Table of Authorities | Sets the appearance of Tables of Authorities. |

### To set up Preferences

1. Select File, Select Preferences; then choose from the options available on the pull-down menu (depending on which preferences you want to set) to open the proper dialog box.

2. Select the area of the dialog box in which you want to make changes.

3. Type new settings or information in the text boxes next to options or settings.

4. Select and deselect options by clicking the check boxes of the items. If an X appears in a check box, the option is turned on.

5. Access pull-down menus by clicking a button while holding down the left mouse button. Move the mouse to highlight the option you want; then release the mouse button.

6. Click the up-down arrow key symbol next to a text box or button to see a menu of options from which to choose; then highlight your choice. Use the scroll bar on the list to look through the menu items.

7. Select OK or Save in dialog boxes that contain these buttons. Your new choices are accepted and the dialog box closes.

   You also can press Enter to accept choices and close the box.

   Select Close or Cancel or press Esc to back out of a dialog box without making changes.

# Print Cartridges and Fonts

### Purpose

Adds printer fonts, cartridges, and print wheels supported by your particular printer. Also adds downloadable soft fonts contained in third-party font packages through WordPerfect's Cartridges and Fonts feature.

### Reminders

You must select a printer in the Select Printer dialog box before you can use this feature.

Auto Code Placement does not act on font changes. The font change takes effect where you have your insertion point. The new font is used for all text until you change fonts again.

### To designate fonts and cartridges

1. Select File, Select Printer. The Select Printer dialog box opens.

2. Click the WordPerfect Printer Drivers check box. An X appears in the check box to show that the option is turned on.

3. Select the printer for which you want to install cartridges and fonts.

4. Click the Setup button to open the Printer Setup dialog box.

5. Select Cartridges/Fonts to see a list of font sources supported by your printer. The Cartridges/Fonts dialog box opens.

6. Select the type of font source you want to modify by highlighting it.

7. Click the Select button to open the Font Groups dialog box.

8. Highlight the group containing the font you want to mark; then choose OK . The Cartridges/Fonts dialog box returns to the screen.

9. Select the cartridge or print wheel you want to use by highlighting it; then select Present When Print Job Begins(*) or Can be Loaded/Unloaded During Job (+) to mark it.

10. Repeat step 9 for every font group you want to include.

11. Select the Select button to select your marked choices; then select Close to return to the Printer Setup dialog box.

12. Select OK  to save your settings and return to the Select Printer dialog box.

13. Select the Update button to update your printer driver with the new fonts; then select Select to select your updated driver. The dialog box closes and you return to the document.

14. Select the Select button to install your new fonts; then select Close to return to the Printer Setup dialog box.

    You can choose another font source to modify as in steps 7 through 11 and then close the Cartridges/ Fonts dialog box.

15. Select OK  to close the Printer Setup dialog box and return to the Printer Select dialog box.

16. Select Update to update your printer driver; then select Select to select the updated printer driver. The dialog box closes and you return to the document.

    When you mark a cartridge, font, or print wheel with an asterisk (*), the Available column in the Cartridges/Fonts dialog box notes a decrease in the quantity available. Quantity refers to the number of slots available for cartridges, memory free in the printer for soft fonts, or number of print wheels on hand.

### *To update Font Quantity when you increase printer memory*

1. Select File, Select Printer to open the Select Printer dialog box.

   Alternatively, press Alt +F , L to call up the dialog box.

2. Highlight the printer you want to modify, and then select Setup.

3. Select Cartridges/Fonts to display font sources.

4. Highlight the font source you want to modify.

5. Select Quantity and enter the new quantity number.

6. Select OK to confirm your choice.

7. Select Close to return to the Printer Setup dialog box.

8. Select Update to update the printer driver.

9. Choose Select. The selected printer is now the current printer.

   If you have installed a font package, the following instructions let you tell WordPerfect how to access the fonts it contains.

### *To set up downloadable soft fonts for your printer*

1. Select File, Select Printer to open the Select Printer dialog box.

2. Select your printer driver.

3. Select Setup.

4. Type a path name for your downloadable font files if you haven't already specified it in Preferences, Location of Files.

5. Select OK to confirm your choice and return to the Select Printer dialog box.

6. Select Update to update the printer driver.

7. Choose Select. The selected printer is now the current printer.

### *To change fonts*

1. From the Font menu, select Font or press $F9$ to call up a dialog box.

2. From the Font List, choose a font by clicking it. The new font is highlighted.

3. Select appearance attributes such as bold.

4. Select OK to confirm your choice to return to your document.

### *Notes*

You can specify the path name for your downloadable fonts in Preferences, Location of Files on the File menu. Then, if you add another font package, you can switch to the new font directory by using the steps in this section for setting up soft fonts.

If your add-on fonts package is DOS-based and you used it with WordPerfect 5.1, select a WordPerfect printer. If you are using a Windows font package such as Facelift or Adobe Type Manager for Windows, select a Windows printer.

When you mark a cartridge, font or print wheel with an asterisk (*), the Available column in the Cartridges/Fonts dialog box notes a decrease in the quantity available. Quantity refers to the number of slots available for cartridges, memory available in the printer for soft fonts, or number of print wheels on hand.

You can specify the path name for downloadable fonts in Preferences, Location of Files, which is on the File menu. Then if you add another font package, you can switch to the new font directory by using the preceding steps for setting up soft fonts.

Auto Code Placement does not act on font changes. The font change takes effect at the location of the insertion point. The new font is used for all text from that point forward until you change fonts again.

If your add-on fonts package is DOS-based and you used it with WordPerfect 5.1, select a WordPerfect printer. If you are using a Windows font package, such as Facelift or Adobe Type Manager for Windows, select a Windows printer. To add these fonts to your font list, use Printer Setup.

See also *Printer Setup* and *Ruler*.

# Print Preview

### *Purpose*

Shows you what the document will look like when it is printed, including graphics (if your monitor can display them).

### *To preview a document*

1. Position the insertion point where you want to begin viewing the document.

2. Select File, Print Preview or press Shift+F5.

3. Select a viewing option from the Button Bar, such as Zoom or 200%.

   If the option you want isn't on the Button Bar, select it from one of the menus.

4. Select File, Print to print the document. You return to the editing screen after the file is sent to the printer.

5. Select Close to return to your document without printing the file.

### *Print Preview Menu Options*

You can choose from the following Preview options from the Print Preview menu:

| *Option* | *Function* |
| --- | --- |
| Zoom | Enables you to examine the document or a certain area of the document more closely. You can zoom in for a close-up look or zoom out to view the document as a whole. |
| Pages | Determines the display. You can select Full Page, Facing Pages, Previous Page, and Next Page. You also can select Go to Page to move to a particular portion of the document quickly. |
| Help | Offers the full range of Help features: Index, Glossary, How Do I?, What Is?, Keyboard, and Using Help. |
| Reset | Resets the default of 100% and redraws the screen after you finish using one of the other options. |
| Button Bar | By default, appears along the side of the window with buttons for selecting viewing options. |
| Button Bar Setup | Enables you to configure a custom Button Bar for Print Preview. This option works like the Button Bar Setup in the editing window. |
| Print | Prints your document and returns you to the editing window. This option is located on the File menu. |
| Close | Closes Print Preview and returns you to the editing window without printing. |

# Printer Select

### Purpose

Enables you to select a printer and to specify whether the printer is a WordPerfect printer driver or a Windows printer driver. Also lets you switch printers.

### Note

If you are using the keyboard rather than the mouse, you must select **Add** after you highlight the printer you want to add.

### To select a WordPerfect printer

1. Select File, Select Printer. The Select Printer dialog box opens.

2. Select WordPerfect Printer Drivers by clicking the check box. The option is selected if an X appears in the check box.

3. Select Add. The Add Printer dialog box opens.

4. Select Printer Files (*.prs).

5. Select your printer from the list that appears by double-clicking the mouse. You return to the Select Printer dialog box.

6. Choose Select. The printer selection is confirmed and you return to the document window.

### Select Printer dialog box options

The following options are available in the Select Printer dialog box.

| Option | Action |
|--------|--------|
| Add | Adds a printer from the list of available printers. |
| Close | Closes the Printer Select dialog box without making changes. |
| Copy | Makes a copy of your printer driver with a slightly different name. You then can edit the printer driver with the PTR.EXE program to add fonts or paper sizes. Then switch between the printer drivers, according to the project you have on hand. |
| Delete | Deletes a printer driver from the list of available printers. |
| Info | Provides information on the currently selected printer. |
| Select | Enables you to select the printer you want to use. |
| Setup | Opens the Printer Setup dialog box. |
| Update | Enables you to update to a newer driver for your printer. |

### To select a Windows printer

1. Select Files, Printer, Select. The Select Printer dialog box opens.

2. Select Windows Printer Drivers by clicking the check box. The option is selected if an X appears in the check box.

3. Double-click your Windows printer from the list that appears.

4. Choose Select to confirm your printer.

### Notes

If you want to use a Windows Font package, such as Facelift or Adobe Type Manager, select the Windows printer driver. The Windows printer driver is very slow, however, and it does not let you choose more than one paper type or size for a document.

You can select a Windows printer without exiting WordPerfect. See your Windows Manual if you haven't yet installed a printer in Windows.

# Printer Setup

### Purpose

Enables you to change printer settings, select cartridges and fonts, change your initial font, change the port destination, and select a sheet feeder and bin number if your printer is equipped with a sheet feeder. You also can use the Printer Setup dialog box to set up a network printer.

### Reminder

If you change the port destination to print to a file on disk, be sure to change it back after printing. Otherwise, all print jobs continue to print to that file.

### To set up your printer

1. Select Files, Select Printer. The Select Printer dialog box opens.

2. Select Setup. The Printer Setup dialog box opens.

3. Change settings as required.

4. Select OK to confirm your choices.

*Note*

See also *Print Fonts*, *Printer Select*, and *Printing*.

# Printing

*Purpose*

Prints a document, using the settings you select for your printer and fonts.

*To print a document*

1. Select Files, Print or press F5. The Print dialog box opens.

2. Change settings as required.

3. Select Print to print the document.

*Print dialog box options*

The Print dialog box contains the following options:

| Option | Function |
|--------|----------|
| Full Document | Prints the entire document. |
| Current Page | Prints the page displayed on-screen. |
| Multiple Pages | Opens the Multiple Pages dialog box so that you can specify the page numbers to print. |
| Document On Disk | Opens the Document On Disk dialog box so that you can type the file name for a document saved on disk. It then prints the document without opening the document. |

| *Option* | *Function* |
|---|---|
| Selected Text | Prints selected text and graphics in the document. |
| Binding Offset | Lets you specify an offset, in inches, for a document you intend to bind into a folder. The offset allows a wider margin area for hole punches. |
| Graphics Quality | Offers a choice of High, Medium, Draft, or Do Not Print. High gives the best graphics resolution; Draft is faster but a lower quality. |
| Text Quality | Offers the same choices as graphics. |
| Number of Copies | Enables you to specify the number of copies to print. |
| Generated by | Enables you to specify whether the print job is to be generated by WordPerfect or your printer. |
| Download Fonts | Displays a dialog box with a Yes/No prompt to ask whether you want to proceed with this option. If you answer Yes, soft fonts are downloaded to your printer (if they are available). |
| Select | Takes you to Select Printer so that you can choose another printer driver. |
| Print | Prints the document according to your current Print dialog box settings. |
| Close | Closes the Print dialog box without printing the document. |

### To set print preferences

1. Select File, Preferences, Print. The Print Settings dialog box opens.

2. Change options as appropriate for your documents.

3. Select OK to accept your choices and close the box.

### Print Settings dialog box options

The Print Settings dialog box contains the following options:

| Option | Function |
|--------|----------|
| Number of Copies | Enables you to specify how many copies to print. |
| Binding Offset | Sets the distance in inches from the left edge of the paper to the start of printed text on the page for binding allowance. |
| Text Quality | Determines the appearance of printed text. |
| Graphics Quality | Determines the resolution of graphics. |
| Redline Method | Enables you to specify appearance and placement of Redline markings. |
| Size Attribute Ratio | Enables you to set the size of the font used for font attributes as a percentage of the current font. Very Large, for example, could be 200% larger than the regular font if you want it twice the normal size. |
| Multiple Copies | Enables you to set the number of copies to be printed of the document or portions of the document. |

| Option | Function |
| --- | --- |
| Generated By | Enables you to specify whether WordPerfect or your printer will produce multiple copies (if your printer supports this option). |

*Notes*

Include a Print button on your Button Bar so that you can print a document with a single mouse click.

You also can set up print settings in Preferences. These settings are permanent, but you can temporarily override them for individual documents by specifying settings in the Print dialog box.

When WordPerfect generates the copies, it creates enough copies of the print job to meet the number you set, and then sends them to the printer. This method produces a print job where the papers are all collated, but it takes longer to print. If your printer supports multiple copies, WordPerfect sends one print job to the printer and tells it to make a set number of copies. Pages are not collated in this case, but print time is faster.

# Redline and Strikeout

*Purpose*

Shows where text is to be inserted or deleted by displaying it with distinctive markings. Redline shows where text is to be inserted; strikeout displays text overwritten with a dashed line to show where it is to be deleted.

The Redline and Strikeout menu options are used in combination with the Document Compare feature to show how one document differs from the other by displaying inserted and deleted text with distinctive markings.

You can set up permanent redline appearance attributes in Preferences.

### Reminder

If you set up redline appearance in the Print Settings dialog box, these settings are always used, unless you override them in the Document Redline dialog box for a particular document.

### To create redline text

1. Select Font, Redline. This menu option turns on markings.

2. Type the text you want redlined.

3. Select Font, Redline again to turn off the markings.

### To change the appearance of redline markings

1. Select Layout, Document, Redline Method. The Document Redline dialog box opens.

2. Change appearance options, if necessary. You can select the location for the markings and the character used to show them.

3. Select OK to accept your choice.

### To set up redline appearance preferences

1. Select File, Preferences, Print. The Print Settings dialog box opens.

2. Change redline appearance settings, if necessary.

3. Select OK to accept your choice.

### *To create strikeout text*

1. Select Font, Strikeout. This menu option turns on strikeout markings.

2. Type the text you want marked with Strikeout.

3. Select Font, Strikeout again to turn off the markings.

### *To delete redline and strikeout markings*

1. Select Tools, Document Compare, Remove Markings. The Remove Markings dialog box opens.

2. Select or deselect Leave Redline Markings, depending on whether or not you want to leave the redlined text in when you delete the strikeout text. The option is on if an X appears in the check box.

3. Select OK To accept your choice.

### *Note*

The appearance of redlining in a document depends on your printer. Some printers display redline as a mark in the margin next to the redlined text. Other printers show redlined text as highlighted or shaded. Color printers can show redlined text in red. On a color monitor, the text between the Redline codes appears in red.

# Retrieving Files

### *Purpose*

Retrieves a file into a document.

### Reminder

The last four documents you save are listed by file name on the File menu. You can retrieve one of these by clicking the file name.

### To retrieve a file

1. Select File, Retrieve. The Retrieve File dialog box opens.

2. Type the name of the file to retrieve and select Retrieve or press Enter. You also can double-click the file name in the Files list.

### To retrieve a file into another file

1. Position the insertion point where you want to place the new file in the document.

2. Select File, Retrieve.

3. Type the name of the file to retrieve and select Retrieve or press Enter. You also can simply double-click the file name in the Files list.

### To retrieve a file in FileManager

1. Select File, FileManager, Files List.

2. Quadruple-click a file name to retrieve it into a new document window.

### Note

The quickest way to retrieve a file is to use the Retrieve File dialog box. In addition to Retrieve, it offers options to change from the default directory, convert a file from a different format to WordPerfect format, view a file, or display the Quick List.

# Reveal Codes

### Purpose

Shows you what formatting codes are inserted into a document and where they are located.

### To delete formatting using Reveal Codes

1. Select View, Reveal Codes or press Alt+F3.

   The screen splits into two parts. Both parts contain the same text, but the bottom half also shows the hidden formatting codes, which are enclosed in brackets.

2. Position the insertion point on the code you want to delete and click the left mouse button once.

3. The code you selected is now highlighted. To delete it, press Del.

4. Select View, Reveal Codes or press Alt+F3 again to close Reveal Codes.

### Notes

WordPerfect for Windows is a WYSIWYG (what you see is what you get) word processor, so codes are not visible on-screen while you are typing unless you use Reveal Codes.

The fastest way to use Reveal Codes is to assign it to a button on the Button Bar.

See also *Button Bar*.

# Ruler

### Purpose

Helps you make fast formatting changes during editing. You can use the Ruler to perform functions such as setting up columns and tables, selecting fonts, and formatting text.

### To set or change tabs

1. Select View, Ruler or press Alt+Shift+F3.

2. Position the insertion point where you want to place the new tab settings.

3. Click a tab marker on the Ruler and drag it to the new position. Release the mouse button when the marker is in place.

4. Use the following techniques to set or change tabs:

   • Delete a tab by clicking it and dragging it below the Ruler.

   • Add a tab by dragging one of the tab markers to any position on the Ruler.

   • Change any tab to a dot leader tab by pressing the button next to the tab pictures on the Ruler; this step displays the dot leader tabs. Then drag a tab marker to the Ruler.

### To reset left and right margins

Drag the margin markers along Ruler to their new positions.

You also can double-click a margin marker to open the Margins dialog box. If you use this method, you can set the top and bottom margins at the same time. You then enter the margins in the text boxes and select OK.

### To change line spacing

1. Click the Line Spacing button on the Ruler while holding down the mouse button. The Line Spacing button is marked with a number such as 1.0 (if you have line spacing set to 1).

2. Use the mouse to highlight the line spacing you want in the pull-down menu; release the mouse button.

   The number on the button now reflects the new line spacing.

   You also can double-click the Line Spacing button on the Ruler to display the Line Spacing dialog box. Then specify line spacing in the dialog box.

### To set justification

1. Click the Justification button on the Ruler while holding down the Mouse button. The Mouse button is marked L, R, F, or C, depending on whether justification is currently set at Left, Right, Full, or Center.

2. Highlight the new justification setting in the pull-down menu and release the mouse button.

### To change fonts

1. Click the Font button on the Ruler and hold down the mouse button.

2. Highlight the new font and release the mouse button.

### To assign fonts to the Font button

1. Double-click the Font button on the Ruler. You also can select Font, Font or press F9.

   The Font Selection dialog box appears.

2. Select Assign to Ruler. Another dialog box appears.

3. From the Font List, click a font to select it. The new font is highlighted.

   You also can double-click a font to add it to the Ruler Font menu automatically. If you select a font this way, skip steps 4 through 7.

4. Click the Add button to add the font to the Ruler Font pull-down menu. Continue to highlight and add as many fonts as you like.

5. Select OK to confirm your choice. You return to the first dialog box.

6. Check the assigned fonts list to make sure that you added all the fonts you want on the list.

7. Select OK to accept your choice. The dialog box closes and you return to your document.

*To create a table*

1. Position the insertion point where you want to start a table.

2. Click the Table button on the Ruler while holding down the mouse button. The Table button contains grid markings.

3. Drag the mouse through the grid to highlight as many columns and rows as you want in the table.

4. Release the mouse button. The table appears in the document at the location of the insertion point.

*To set up columns*

1. Click the Columns button on the Ruler while holding down the mouse button. The Columns button contains horizontal lines that look like newspaper columns.

2. Use the mouse to highlight the number of columns you want to set up. Release the mouse button.

   The text now lines up in columns.

*Notes*

Settings that you make with the Ruler affect only the
current document. You can, however, change several of
the default Ruler options by selecting File, Preferences,
Environment and making selections in the dialog box.

The Ruler is designed to work with normal WYSIWYG
display; when used with Draft Mode, the characters do
not display accurately with the Ruler measurements.
You must either turn off Draft Mode when you use the
Ruler, or preview the document using Print Preview.

If Auto Code Placement is turned on, the changes you
make with the Ruler buttons are placed at the beginning
of the paragraph you are in when you make the changes.
These changes affect all text that follows until you
change the settings again. Auto Code Placement does
not act on font changes, however. The font change
takes effect at the location of the insertion point or on
a selected passage of text. The new font is used for all
text, from the insertion point forward, until you change
fonts again.

Make sure that you have set File, Preferences,
Environment to have tabs snapped to the Ruler grid
before trying to adjust margins with the Ruler.
Otherwise, you cannot use the Ruler to adjust margins.

# Save As

*Purpose*

Enables you to save your document with a new name, in
a new format, or in a different directory from the default
directory.

*To use Save As*

1. Retrieve a document or create a new one. Select Save
   As using one of the following methods:

- Click the Save As button on the Button Bar.

- Select File menu, Save As by clicking with the mouse.

- Press F3.

The Save As dialog box appears.

2. In the text box, type the drive and directory (if different than the default) and the new file name.

3. To save the file in a different format, click the small arrow next to the File Format text box and select the format you want to use.

4. Select Save or press Enter to save the new file.

*Notes*

Selecting Save replaces the original copy of a file on your drive with the document on your screen, if the two files have the same name. Save As enables you to rename the on-screen document so that you retain the earlier version while saving the new one.

# Search and Replace

*Purpose*

Enables you to find and replace text and codes in documents.

*To search and replace text or codes*

1. Position the insertion point where you want to begin the search.

2. Select Edit, Search or press F2. The Search dialog box opens.

3. Specify options, including whether to search forward or backward.

4. If you are searching for text, type the text in the Search For text box.

5. If you are searching for a code, select Codes and scan the codes list. Highlight the code you want to find and select Insert to insert it into the Search text box.

   Search begins and stops at the first occurrence of the item for which you are looking.

6. Select Search Next (Shift+F2) or Search Previous (Alt+F2) to see other appearances of the text or code.

7. If you want to replace the text or code for which you are searching, select Edit, Replace or press Ctrl+F2. The Replace dialog box appears.

8. In the Replace dialog box, type the text you want to replace and the replacement text.

   If you are replacing a code, select Codes. Scan the codes list, highlight the replacement code, and select Insert to insert it into the Replace text box.

9. Select Replace to replace one instance of the text; select Replace All to replace all occurrences of the text.

---

*Note*

To delete all occurrences of specified text, type the text to replace in the appropriate text box and leave the replacement text box blank. Then select Replace.

# Select

---

*Purpose*

Selects or defines a portion of your text for an action such as deleting, moving, copying, or enhancing with

boldface or underlining. Selected text appears
highlighted.

### To use a mouse to select text

1. Position the insertion point at the beginning of the
   text you want to select.

2. Hold down the left mouse button and move the
   insertion point through the text until you highlight all
   the text that you want to select.

3. Release the mouse button. The text is selected and
   highlighted.

   To deselect text, position the insertion point anywhere in the selected text and click the left mouse
   button once.

   To delete selected text, press Del.

### To use other mouse methods to select text

You also can use other mouse techniques to select text.
Position the insertion point on the text that you want to
select, and use these methods:

- Double-click to select a word.

- Triple-click to select a sentence.

- Quadruple-click to select a paragraph.

- Press Shift and click the mouse button to select text
  from the insertion point to the position of the mouse
  pointer.

### To use the keyboard to select text

You also can use the keyboard to select text. Position the
insertion point on the text that you want to select, and
use these methods:

- Press Shift+→ or Shift+← to select one character to
  the right or left of the insertion point.

- Press **Shift+↑** or **Shift+↓** to select one line above or below the insertion point.

- Press **Shift+End** to select to the end of the line before codes.

### To use Select Mode

1. Press **F8** to turn on Select Mode.

2. Use the cursor keys to move to the end of the area you want to select.

3. Perform operations on the selected text, such as printing, cutting, deleting, or enhancing it.

4. Press **F8** again to turn off Select Mode.

### Note

You also can use Select with block protect to keep the selected text together on a page during editing.

# Sort

### Purpose

Sorts numbers or words in either ascending or descending order.

### To sort document contents

1. Open the document to be sorted.

2. Unless you want to sort the entire document, select text to be sorted.

3. Select Tools, Sort, or press **Ctrl+Shift+F12**. The Sort dialog box opens.

4. Select the record type and sort order.

5. Fill in the key definitions text boxes with the numbers that show WordPerfect the location of the word, field, or cell within the record. WordPerfect needs to know the location of the keywords in order to sort them.

6. To sort on more than one keyword or field, select Insert to insert another key.

7. Select OK to start the sort.

---

### Note

This feature works with lines, paragraphs, rows in a table, or secondary merge records. You can sort items alphabetically or numerically, in ascending or descending order. You might, for example, sort an address list alphabetically by last name, starting with A. For mass mailings, however, you might sort your secondary merge file by ZIP code to take advantage of the discount presort rate.

# Speller

---

### Purpose

Spell checks your entire document. You also can use it to check a particular word, check for certain capitalization errors, and look for duplicate occurrences of a word (such as *the the*).

---

### Reminder

The Speller is a separate application, so you can minimize it to an icon and still keep it active. To minimize the Speller, click the button in the top left corner of the Speller dialog box; then click Minimize. To restore it, double-click the icon.

### *To use Speller*

1. Select Tools, Speller.

2. Click the Document button next to Check while holding down the left mouse button to display the menu. Highlight an option. Release the mouse button after you select the spell checking option that you want (Word, Document, To End of Document, Page, To End of Page, Selected Text, or To End of Selection).

3. To check the spelling of a particular word, type the word in the Word text box.

4. Select Start.

5. If Speller finds a misspelled word, you can select from the following options:

| *Option* | *Function* |
|----------|-----------|
| Replace | Replaces the word with the correctly spelled word. |
| Add | Adds the word to WordPerfect's dictionary. |
| Skip Once | Skips this occurrence of the word. |
| Skip Always | Always skips this spelling of the word. |

6. When the Speller Spell Check Completed dialog box appears, select OK.

7. Select Close to close the Speller and return to your document.

# Spreadsheet Importing

## Purpose

Imports and links spreadsheet files directly from PlanPerfect, Lotus 1-2-3, Microsoft Excel, Quattro, and Quattro Pro.

In addition, Spreadsheet Linking establishes a link between the spreadsheet and the document that updates the document every time you update the spreadsheet. Link Editing enables you to edit an existing link or modify link options.

## To import a spreadsheet file

1. Position the insertion point where you want to import the spreadsheet into the document.

2. Select Tools, Spreadsheet, Import. The dialog box opens.

3. In the text box, type the name of the spreadsheet file to import. Specify table or text, the range of cells to import, and the range name.

4. Select OK to import the spreadsheet and return to your document.

## To link a document to a spreadsheet

1. Position the insertion point where you want to create the link.

2. Select Tools, Spreadsheet, Create Link. The Create Spreadsheet Link dialog box opens.

3. Type the spreadsheet file name in the text box.

   You also can click the List button to the right of the text box. A list of files appears, and you can double-click the file you want.

4. Designate the type, range, and range name.

5. Select OK to confirm your selection. WordPerfect inserts the link and imports the spreadsheet, and you return to the document.

### To edit a link

1. Position the insertion point between the [Link] and [Link End] codes.

2. Select Tools, Spreadsheet, Edit Link.

3. Make any required changes.

4. Select OK to update the link and import the new data.

### To update links

You can use one of the following methods to update links:

- Select Tools, Spreadsheet, Update All Links to update all your links.

- Select Tools, Spreadsheet, Link Options to select Update on Retrieve. When you select this option, links are updated automatically when you retrieve the document.

### Notes

When you import a spreadsheet into WordPerfect, you copy that spreadsheet and its data into a WordPerfect document.

When you link a WordPerfect document to a spreadsheet, the data in the document is updated whenever you update the spreadsheet data.

# Starting WordPerfect

### *Purpose*

Starts WordPerfect for Windows.

### *Reminder*

When you ran the Install program, WordPerfect for Windows installed itself in Windows.

### *To start WordPerfect for Windows*

1. Start Windows and look for the WordPerfect icon.

2. Double-click the icon. A window appears with four icons. One of these is WordPerfect. The others are for FileManager, Speller, and Thesaurus.

3. Double-click the WordPerfect icon to start the program.

# Styles

### *Purpose*

Enable you to create and use styles. Styles are special files you can write that include formatting codes and text that affect your document. Like macros, they perform their magic instantly.

You use styles to format an entire document, or to perform a specific formatting function, such as applying boldface, underlining, and centering to a heading. You can save a style to a style library after you create it so that you can use it on other documents.

Open styles remain in effect throughout the document. Paired styles can be turned on at a certain point in your text and then off again as you type.

### To retrieve styles

1. Position the insertion point where you want to start styles or select the text to which you want to apply a style.

2. Select Layout, Styles; select the Styles button on the Button Bar; or press Alt+F8. The Styles dialog box opens.

3. If no styles are visible in the list portion of the dialog box, select Retrieve. WordPerfect retrieves the styles in LIBRARY.STY and displays their descriptions.

4. Select the style you want by clicking it to highlight it.

5. Select the On button to turn on the highlighted style.

6. Close the dialog box.

### To create a style

1. Select Layout, Styles, or press Alt+F8. The Styles dialog box appears.

2. Click the Create button to open the Style Properties dialog box.

3. In the  appropriate text boxes, type the name and description of the style and indicate whether it is to be a paired or open style.

4. If you are creating a paired style, click the Enter Key Inserts button to define how the style acts.

5. Select OK to confirm your choice. The Create Style editing screen appears.

6. Select the format commands you want to include, such as Font, Line Spacing, Margins, and so on. You select these commands the same way that you select them from the document window.

7. Select the Properties button if you want to make changes to the properties of the style you are editing. The Style Properties dialog box appears.

8. Select OK to confirm the properties changes. You return to the Styles Editor.

9. Close the editing screen when you finish creating your style.

10. Click the Save button to save the new style.

The new style is now listed in the Styles dialog box and in the Styles pull-down menu on the Ruler.

### To use a style

1. If you want the style applied to the whole document, position the insertion point at the beginning of the document.

2. Select text to which you want to apply a paired on/off style if you only want to use a style on a certain section of the text, such as a heading.

3. From the Ruler, select Styles. Hold down the mouse button and move the mouse to highlight your style choice; then release the mouse button.

4. Turn on Reveal Codes; you see the Style codes.

### To edit a style

1. Select Layout, Styles, or press Alt+F8. The Styles dialog box appears.

2. Highlight the style you want to edit.

3. Click the Edit button to open the Styles Edit dialog box.

4. Make any changes.

5. Select Close to save changes and return to the document.

*Note*

> Paired styles are turned on and off around selected text.
> An open style is turned on and stays on until you turn it
> off again.

# Tab Set

*Purpose*

> Sets left tabs, right tabs, center tabs, decimal tabs, and
> dot leader tabs, starting where you want them in the
> document and spaced as you specify.

*To set tab stops*

1. Select Layout, Line, Tab Set, or press Shift+F9 and
   select Tab Set. The Tab Set dialog box opens, and it
   displays the current tab settings.

2. Select Clear All Tabs to set all new tabs or select
   Clear Tab to change one tab.

3. In the Position text box, type a new tab setting. You
   also can select a setting from the list box.

4. From the Tab list on the left side of the dialog box,
   click the box next to the type of tab you want.

5. Click the Set Tab button.

6. Set as many tabs and types of tabs as you need.

7. Select OK to confirm your changes.

*Note*

> You can change back to the default Tab Set at any time
> by returning to the Layout, Line, Tab Stop dialog box
> and clicking the Default button.

# Table of Authorities

*Purpose*

Lists reference citations for a legal brief.

To create a Table of Authorities, you mark the authorities, define each section of the table, and generate the table.

*To place the table at the beginning of the document*

1. Position the insertion point at the beginning of the document.

2. Press **Ctrl+Enter** to generate a hard page break.

3. Move the insertion point above the page break to the beginning of the clean page.

4. Type a heading, then press **Enter** several times to insert some blank spaces between the heading and the first section.

5. Select Tools, Define, Table of Authorities, or press **Shift+F12** and select Table of Authorities.

6. Select the number of the section to be defined. You must define each section separately.

7. Set up format options and select **OK** to confirm your choice.

8. Specify a new number for the page that follows the Table of Authorities.

   Skipping this step may result in inaccurate page references because generating the table may insert new pages into the document. The new page number setting causes WordPerfect to renumber the pages correctly and automatically.

9. Select Tools, Generate, or press **Alt+F12** to generate the first section of the table. Repeat steps 5 through 9 until all sections are generated.

*Note*

You can divide a Table of Authorities into sections for the different types of citations with a different format for each. WordPerfect lets you define up to 16 sections for a Table of Authorities. Determine what sections to include and the order of their appearance before you begin marking text. Typical sections might include cases, statutory provisions, rules, and so on.

# Table of Contents

*Purpose*

Generates a table of contents for a document.

To create a table of contents, you mark the text to be included, define the list as a table of contents, and generate the table.

### To mark the text for the table of contents

1. Select the first item and press **F12**. The Mark Text dialog box opens.

2. Select the level number (up to **5**) for the table of contents. For example, you want might want to use chapter headings for level 1 and subheadings for level 2.

3. Continue marking until you include all text for the table of contents.

### To place the table of contents at the beginning of the document

1. Position the insertion point at the beginning of the document.

2. Press **Ctrl+Enter** to generate a hard page break.

3. Move the insertion point to the page above the page break.

4. Type a title and press **Enter** several times to separate the title from the list.

---

### *To define the table of contents*

1. Select Tools, Define, Table of Contents, or press **Shift+F12** and select Table of Contents. The Define Table of Contents dialog box opens.

2. Select the number of levels you want in the table.

3. Select from five numbering styles. You can select from the following styles:

| | |
|---|---|
| 1. No Numbering | No page numbers |
| 2. Text # | Page number follows item |
| 3. Text [#] | Page number in ( ) follows item |
| 4. Text   # | Flush right page numbers |
| 5. Text.....# | Flush right page numbers with dot leaders |

4. Select **OK** to confirm your choices and close the Define dialog box.

---

### *To set a new page number*

1. Position the insertion point just below the page break.

2. Select Layout, Page, Numbering.

3. Type the new page number in the New Page Number text box.

4. Select **OK** to confirm your choice.

### To generate the Table of Contents

1. Position the insertion point under the Table of Contents title at the point where you want the table of contents to appear.

2. Press Alt+F12 to generate the table.

   WordPerfect generates the Table of Contents with the page numbers where those headings can be found.

### Note

If you later make changes and additions in your document, you must regenerate the table of contents so that it contains the updated, accurate page numbers.

# Tables

### Purpose

Enables you to set up tables to organize items by columns and rows without having to calculate tab settings.

### To create a table

1. Position the insertion point where you want the table to begin.

2. Select Layout, Tables, Create, or press Ctrl+F9 and select Create. The Create Table dialog box appears.

3. In the appropriate text boxes, enter the number of rows and columns for the table.

4. Select OK. The dialog box closes and you return to the document.

You now can begin entering information into the table. Use Tab to move to the next cell in the row.

### To select table options

1. Position the insertion point inside the table.

2. Select Layout, Tables, Options, or press Ctrl+F9 and select Options. The Table Options dialog box opens.

3. Change the settings, if necessary.

4. Select OK to accept the settings and return to the document.

### To change the lines around a cell or group of cells

1. Position the insertion point in the table.

2. Select Layout, Tables, Lines, or press Ctrl+F9 and select Lines. The Table Lines dialog box opens.

3. Select a line type for the left, right, bottom, top, inside, or outside lines of the cells by clicking the button next to those positions and dragging the mouse to highlight your choice. Select None if you want invisible lines.

4. Select OK to confirm and save your choice and return to the table.

### To insert columns and rows in a table

1. Position the insertion point at the position where you want to add a cell in the table.

2. Select Layout, Tables, Insert, or press Ctrl+F9 and select Insert.

3. Select Columns or Rows.

4. Specify how many columns (or rows) you want to add at the insertion point in your table.

5. Select OK to confirm your choice.

### To delete columns or rows in a table

1. Position the insertion point in the row or column you want to delete.

2. Select Layout, Tables, Delete, or press **Ctrl+F9** and select Delete. The Delete Columns/Rows dialog box opens.

3. Click either the Columns or Rows check box, depending on what you want to delete.

4. In the text box, enter the number of columns (or rows) that you want to delete.

5. Select **OK** to confirm your choice.

### To join cells

1. Select the cells to be joined by dragging the mouse over them to highlight them.

2. Select Layout, Tables, Join, or press **Ctrl+F9** and select Join.

   When you return to the document, the two smaller cells are now one big cell.

### To split cells

1. Position the insertion point in the cell you want to divide.

2. Select Layout, Tables, Split, or press **Ctrl+F9** and select Split. The Split Column/Row dialog box opens.

3. Type the number of the column or row that you want to split the cell into.

4. Select **OK** to confirm your choice.

# Thesaurus

## *Purpose*

Enables you to look up synonyms and antonyms in a flash without having to leave your document—a very handy tool for improving your writing.

## *To use the Thesaurus*

1. Select Tools, Thesaurus, or press Alt+F1. The Thesaurus dialog box appears.

2. In the Word text box, type the word you need to look up.

3. Click the Look Up button.

4. Scroll up and down the list of displayed words to see what word most nearly expresses your meaning. Click the word to highlight it.

5. Click Replace to replace the original word with the new word.

6. Close the dialog box to return to your document.

## *Note*

You also can highlight any word in the list box to place it in the Word window and look it up.

# Upper- and Lowercase

## *Purpose*

Converts uppercase letters to lowercase and vice versa.

### To convert case

1. Select the word, phrase, or passage you want to change.

2. Select Edit, Convert Case and select Upper or Lowercase.

   All highlighted text is converted to the case you select.

3. Click the insertion point anywhere in the highlighted text to turn off the highlighting.

# Word Count

### Purpose

Automatically counts the words in your document.

### To use Word Count

1. Select Tools, Word Count.

   A dialog box appears that shows the number of words in the document.

2. Select OK to return to your document.

# WP Characters

### Purpose

Offers some special characters to insert into your document. The characters are not available on the keyboard.

### *To add WordPerfect characters to your document*

1. Position the insertion point at the place in your document where you want the special character to appear.

2. Select Font, WP Characters. The WP Characters dialog box appears.

3. Click the Set Button so that you can select a character set. Hold down the left mouse button to highlight your choice of sets. Release the mouse button and the new character set appears.

4. Click one of the displayed characters.

5. Select Insert to insert the character into your document.

6. Select Close to close the dialog box. You return to your document.

### *Note*

See your WordPerfect for Windows Reference Manual for a descriptive listing of the available characters and symbols.

# Index